The Wo

TREVOR BARNES w
in 1951 and w
Grammar School and Pembroke College,
Oxford where he read modern languages.

He is a freelance journalist and radio
reporter for B.B.C. Radio current affairs
and religious programmes. Over the past
six years he has reported regularly for
Radio 4's "Sunday" programme, and
made numerous radio documentaries on a
wide range of issues.

He is married and lives in Guildford.

TREVOR BARNES

The Wounded City

Collins
FOUNT PAPERBACKS

First published in Great Britain by
Fount Paperbacks, London in 1987

Made and printed in Great Britain by
William Collins Sons & Co. Ltd, Glasgow

To my parents
and
in memory of Gabriel

Contents

Introduction

On a shelf in one corner of the staff rest room in the Accident and Emergency Unit of the Royal Victoria Hospital in Belfast stands an unremarkable looking row of magazines. From a distance it looks for all the world like a collection of volumes of *Country Life*. Closer inspection reveals the error. For instead of a line of books recording the untroubled pattern of rural life across the water, what you have here is a series of professional medical journals whose very title provides you with a fairly accurate metaphor for everyday life in far from untroubled Belfast. *The Journal of Trauma* is its name (its subject: the treatment of violent physical injury), and although it is far from being the city's official guidebook it could, in name at least, be Belfast's own, suggesting as it does the well-thumbed chronicle of shock — mental, spiritual and physical — delivered daily to an already wounded city.

"When somebody's been shot with a handgun what you see is a little hole either side. It looks as if you've got a little tunnel running from one to the other — much the same as if you'd put a skewer right through and pulled it out. But the difference between the bullet and skewer is that the bullet has a tremendous amount of energy which it transmits to the tissue around in the form of a blast wave. Now rifle bullets have an even greater force and if one goes, say, through your femur it'll shatter it into fragments, which will in turn start to move about violently and become, in effect, secondary missiles. They will rip through blood vessels and live tissue and transform it into dead tissue. So if you're hit in the thigh, for example, you may have a tiny hole at the front but the hole at the back will be the size of a soup plate." It is in those straightforward terms that Mr William Rutherford, the Head of the R.V.H.'s emergency unit, will describe the rudimentary detail of the kind of physical trauma he and his team have to deal with every week — all that alongside the road accidents, the rail crashes, the fires and the bewildering litany of domestic and industrial mishaps which make his unit among the busiest, and most highly specialized, in Europe. "Gunshot wounds", he says, "are among the most common of the injuries specifically attributable to civil disturbances."

The most common, perhaps, but far from the only injury eighteen years of "Troubles" have thrown up. Bombs, Mr Rutherford will tell you, have claimed their greedy share of Belfast's wounded too.

"The thing about explosions is that instead of presenting you with three extra patients a day over a year, they give you your casualties at one go. You may have no bomb victims for a month then you'll have eighty within an hour. So part of the problem for us is an organizational one. How do you mobilize doctors and nursing staff? Where can you get your empty beds from? And so on. We deal with explosions much as we would with a railway crash. But there are specific injuries. Bombs throw fragments about and people are peppered with all sorts of things. And, whereas you might be able to leave bits of glass and metal in the body, if you have, say, bits of clothing blown in the wounds then the clean-up is pretty extensive. But, of course, at the same time that people are being peppered there's this great blast wave working on them and that affects especially parts of the body where there are pockets of air. The consequences are found in the lungs, in the intestines, and in the ear. People may be brought from the bombing stone-deaf. Now, some will recover but some won't, and some will be left with balance difficulties or noises in the head. One specific injury is 'blast lung' where the lungs, instead of being light and airy, have become waterlogged through the blast. But we wouldn't normally see that. That's usually only seen by pathologists when the person's dead." So much for physical trauma.

But Belfast's wounds are not only of the flesh but of the heart as well, its trauma both physical and spiritual. You need only glance through the "in memoriam" columns of the *Belfast Telegraph* to get some idea of the scar tissue the wounds leave behind.

Open the paper and most weeks there will be five or six families remembering the death of one man. And often in words that suggest continuing bitterness and hatred: "To————murdered by————" or some similar inscription. There cannot be a single person living in the city who has not been touched by the violence, who has not known a relative, a friend, or an acquaintance injured in some way. As a visitor to Belfast I have experienced it time and again, and some of those people's stories are told in this book. Shopkeepers will tell you of rioting here, house-wives will tell you of a bomb going off there. Schoolchildren speak of older cousins shot and killed, clergymen of parishioners kneecapped – shot in the leg, that is, by a handgun, as a punishment for some misde-meanour. Taxi drivers, business men, shop assistants, teachers – in a word, *everybody* will know of someone injured by gunshots, explosions, stones, flying glass, petrol bombs, or plastic bullets.

Events like that, of course, are not happening all the time, nor are they the only things that take place in Belfast. Ordinary men and women, often in extraordinary circumstances, continue to ensure that life goes on as normal. But violence has been done in the city, and it is a part of people's conscious and subconscious lives in a way that it is nowhere in mainland Britain. Let me give you an illustration. I imagine most of you reading this will, like me, never have handled a gun. A gun is not the sort of thing that comes your way. You may see the odd shotgun slung over a farmer's shoulder. You may see a sportsman at a pistol shoot taking careful aim at a target; the occasional lover of the country life taking pot shots at clay pigeons – all under the most controlled of conditions. But firearms are essentially alien objects, glimpsed only at a safe distance or in the two-dimensional world of film and television fiction. Such is not the case for the people of Belfast.

There are those, for example, who have been handling guns since they were sixteen years old, developing a familiarity with rifles and revolvers in secret weapons training sessions organized by the outlawed paramilitary organizations of both sides. True, they represent a small group – how small it is impossible to gauge – but dismissing them as unimportant in the context of everyday Belfast life is misguided. A young man driven by anger and armed with bricks and bottles may only be troublesome. A callow youth with a cause in his heart and a Luger in his pocket is dangerous.

Then there is a second group who have seen guns in action, either because they were pointed their way by a succession of masked men in a hurry or because they were discharged into their legs, shoulders, backs or faces. Both the gunmen and the victims tell their stories here, as do those from the third and largest group of all – the men and women who have been schooled, albeit reluctantly, to accept that guns and the occasional bomb are part of the street furniture of the city. They have become accustomed to the presence of armed British soldiers on endless foot patrols past endless rows of terraced houses. For some it is a foreign army of occupation waging a war which justifies the use of armed force in retaliation. For others it is the thin red line which keeps barbarity and anarchy at bay. Either way there is the tacit assumption that Belfast is a violent city, where the gun is a proper and legitimate tool to counter the threat of violence which is constantly below the surface of ordinary life, ready at any moment to break cover in the most horrifying and unpredictable of ways.

If I have begun with a grim picture of Belfast it is only by way of describing what sets it apart from other cities in Britain. It is not the whole picture and it is easy enough to get a distorted impression of what goes on there by focusing solely on the violence. Take, for instance, the experience of one Englishman in a story told to me by his Belfast colleague, a fellow lecturer at Queen's University.

The Englishman had a part-time teaching contract at the university requiring him to spend a couple of days each week in the city. The man was nervous, and worked out for himself a careful routine which would be guaranteed to keep him out of danger. It went as follows. He would take the plane from Heathrow to Belfast, and from there hire a taxi to the university. Safe in the taxi he would make his way by the most direct route possible to his lodgings — themselves safe within the university complex. Each day he would cover the short distance to work and return in the evening to the security of his room, as if to a clearing in Belfast's badlands into which he never set foot. When his two days' teaching were up he would hire a taxi for the return journey direct to the airport, where he boarded the plane for Heathrow, doubtless relieved that another ordeal was at an end.

The careful routine lasted for a couple of years, until friends and colleagues suggested that this well-honed strategy for self-preservation was perhaps exaggerated, and that there was another side to Belfast than that of which he had read in the newspapers. The Englishman was not convinced. But his colleagues insisted, and proposed that they all go to town for a drink, perhaps for a meal. Against his instincts he finally agreed, and the four of them set off by car to enjoy what entertainment any normal city could provide. Unfortunately for the Englishman it was an untimely trip. For not only had they chosen the day but also the very moment and the very spot where "Loyalist" gunmen had decided to stage their ambush and assassination of Sinn Fein's leader, Gerry Adams. There was to be no quiet drink for the Englishman's party that day. Instead there was commotion. What they witnessed were shouts, screams, gunshots and injury. The security forces appeared on the scene to restore order, but not before people had been seen running for cover and had been told to spreadeagle themselves on the ground.

Yes, the Englishman had known it all along! Hadn't he always suspected that University Road led directly to the Streets of Laredo? Gerry Adams, though seriously wounded, survived. The Englishman's impressions of Belfast had been dealt a mortal blow. In Belfast it is important to keep everything – war and peace – in perspective.

Belfast is a city not a headline. And it is as easy as it is mistaken to draw hasty conclusions from isolated incidents that take place there. There are art galleries and nightclubs, theatres and markets – all of them doing a fine trade. The city centre is busy and relaxed. Buskers play in the pedestrian precinct while shoppers come and go as they do anywhere else. If you live in the comfortable outer fringes of the city it is possible not to be affected by the trouble at all, possible to read of it all in the newspaper as if it were happening in another city instead of just a few miles down the road. The check points and the green turnstiles which ring the town centre are largely unmanned now. The intense spate of bombings in the mid-seventies has stopped, and by and large people feel more at their ease. But there are signs on the street that the possibility of disturbance is never far away. Take the huge yellow iron barriers at the known trouble spots. They are folded back most of the time, like old-fashioned level crossing gates after the train has gone through, but ready to be unlocked, swung into position across the road and then locked again. The purpose of these is to keep apart one section of the city from another in time of trouble or – as the security forces might

14

see it – to block the march of the warring hordes from both directions.

Northumberland Street, for example, is a short thoroughfare linking (or, more correctly, separating) the Republican Falls Road and the Loyalist Shankill Road. However relaxed the city centre and suburbs may feel, the mere presence of a yellow level crossing barrier on Northumberland Street is a visible reminder that the uneasy peace can be blown apart when the political and tribal temperature starts to rise.

It was not always so, as residents will tell you. Protestants on the Shankill crossed freely to the Falls, and in return the Catholics made full use of the Shankill's shops – well known for their choice and their bargains. But almost two decades of trouble have made folk uneasy, and moving between "Nationalist" and "Loyalist" territory is much rarer now.

A small incident to illustrate Belfast's bizarre divisions. I was in the Shankill one bright Monday morning in May, and late for an appointment I had in the Falls. I called in at a local taxi firm.

"Could I have a cab?"

"Certainly, sir, where to?"

"To St Louise's Comprehensive School on the Falls Road."

"Ah, well, sir. Now, there we've a problem. We can't take you there."

"Why not?"

By this time I was suspecting that unpleasantness lay at the bottom of this as yet unfathomable refusal. I feared some inbuilt prejudice on the driver's behalf towards the stranger, some dormant hostility which awoke when unwelcome outsiders chanced to stray inside. In this I was completely wrong – Belfast is nothing if not hospitable to the traveller.

"The problem is, sir, we might get hijacked." It took a moment to sink in.

"Hijacked on a Monday morning? In broad daylight?"

"Well, you see, we're a Shankill cab firm and anyone can tell that. It mightn't be safe for our boys."

"What about me?" I almost said but didn't.

"It's just to be on the safe side. You'd be better phoning for a city cab. Sit down and I'll phone one for you."

It was an elementary lesson in road safety Belfast-style, and an indication of the strains ordinary people have to contend with every day, in one form or another.

The most tragic reminder, though, is the "Peace Line" built along the border between the Falls and the Shankill. It is a strange euphemism for a twenty-foot-high concrete and corrugated iron wall put up to prevent sectarian incursions, stone throwing, petrol bombing and worse. With physical barriers like the Peace Line, and the notional barriers of politics and religion which stretch back generations, what hope is there that Belfast's wounds will ever heal? What hope that people will live together with justice and in peace?

The stories contained here go some way to show the effort and the sacrifice a few people are putting into finding an answer. They will not solve the problem of Northern Ireland alone – few are foolhardy enough to claim that. The people in these pages represent no one but themselves; they have no grand strategy to implement overnight, and concede that they rely on those with far more power than they have to bring about great changes. As for small changes, however, that is a different matter. Wherever such people as these are to be found some change does occur, and not to see the signs of hope when they look you in the face is as dangerous as it is to ignore advice from well-intentioned cab drivers on bright spring mornings.

A friend of mine from the city warned me of the danger of painting too hopeful a picture. "There's a great hope industry out there", he said with a sigh of cynical resignation. "And where's it got us? People talk of lighting candles in the darkness. But what good are they when what we need is a bloody big power station?"

It is not for an outsider like me to argue with a man who has lived in Belfast all his life, but then that is not the point of this book. It is no more than the account of an outsider; of one more observer who has passed through the city and intends to return; of a visitor privileged to meet men and women whose stories of quiet courage and forgiveness against all the odds cannot fail to impress. That is why I have let them do the talking. They may not have all the answers but without them the solutions would take far longer to find.

When the power station is finally built in Belfast it will be thanks in part to people like these (and there are many more of them) who, in the long chilly years when many said the turbines had all but given up the ghost, have continued – at great personal cost to themselves – to stoke up the fires of love and to generate the warmth of human understanding and Christian compassion.

Victims of Violence

John Kelly

John Kelly is a quiet family man in his mid-fifties, living in East Belfast. He is not the sort of man you would imagine people wanting to murder nor is he the sort of man you would expect to see running for his life through a council estate in broad daylight. But having decided to make a stand and to do his "bit" to help the city, that was precisely the risk he opened himself up to. He has stood by his decision and now lives daily with the consequences.

"For a number of years I had worked in the television trade as an engineer and repair man. Most of my work was on outside rounds in the Turf Lodge area of town."

Turf Lodge is an estate in "Catholic" West Belfast – a place in which a resident of "Protestant" East Belfast would not automatically find it the most comfortable to work. But it did not trouble John Kelly. As a committed Salvationist he was prepared to go where God sent him – even if it was to repair TV sets. He was well known in the area and well liked.

"I met a lot of honest peace-loving people up there, particularly when I used to service the sets in the schools", he says. "They were people I looked upon as friends, who didn't want to be involved in the troubles at all but who were being terrorized really. You know, some fellah – from the Republican paramilitaries – would come to the door and tell them they'd have to hide this gun or whatever. And they had to do it. There was no way they could refuse. And so I felt it was time somebody did something about it. I felt it was time I did my bit but what could I do?"

He decided to join the security forces and that is why the provisional I.R.A. decided to murder him.

"Now it was about this time that I got talking to a Roman Catholic man down in the Markets area. He'd been sitting in my car minding it for me and had just picked up the Salvation Army songbook which I'd left there. When I got back he'd left it open on the seat — and I can remember now the verse he'd been reading:

> In the battle men are needed,
> Men of hope and faith and prayer.

I thought about it for a while and came to the conclusion that there was an answer here. This was definitely guidance from somewhere for me to join up. So I applied to join the part-time volunteer reserve of the Royal Ulster Constabulary. At the time I felt there was an urgent need for men in the force — particularly, I thought, for good Christian people who were not biased against the Catholic population. And certainly I'd worked among them for many years. I applied and was accepted. They told me to go along and have my photograph taken on the Monday night at Connswater so that I could be issued with a warrant card. On the Thursday we were to be issued with our uniforms and we were to start training a fortnight after that."

But it was to be some time before his training did begin. At this time John Kelly had no idea of the shock that was lying in store for him very shortly. A week after he had had his photograph taken he was back in his van on his repair round.

"It was about midday. I was driving down Monagh Road in Turf Lodge approaching a zebra crossing. I noticed two young lads standing there with a couple of kids next to them. There were two cars in front of me. As I got closer I noticed the youths were masked — I reckon they must have been about eighteen or so. They let the two cars pass then pushed the kids out on to the crossing, forcing me to stop. At this point they produced guns and told me they knew I'd joined the R.U.C. They took me at gunpoint to a flat close by in Norglen Parade where there was a third masked man waiting. After they'd searched me two of them went off while the other one stayed with me with a gun to my head. After half an hour they came back in a black taxi and I was driven to the Upper Springfield Road. They pulled in at a bend where it was all sealed off for roadworks and from where we wouldn't be seen. This part of the road was completely out of sight of the estate.

"They bundled me out of the taxi, put the gun to my head and pulled the trigger.

"There was a click. The gun didn't fire. So then I decided to leave – pretty rapidly actually! I went off down the road, over a hedge and across some fields. My idea was to make for a house where I knew somebody would be friendly and where I hoped they'd look after me. Now by this time they'd got their gun sorted out and came running after me firing at me. One round hit me in the hip. At the time I didn't feel much – I thought I'd kicked up a stone while I was running zig-zag fashion across the field. I was beginning to feel very weak now because I'd run quite a distance and at the time I was rather overweight anyway. I realized I wasn't going to make it to where I'd intended. By this time I was running along the back of some houses and this Roman Catholic man came out and caught me as I was falling. He dragged me into his house and closed the door but they broke the door open and shot me again through the right shoulder as I lay there on the kitchen floor. Then they left.

"Now, whether they left because they'd run out of ammunition I don't know – I'd counted roughly five shots. But anyway they did leave, and the man ran out to phone the police and ambulance. He also found the priest had been visiting a couple of doors away and brought him to the scene. I was taken to the R.V.H. and then the police caught up with me there.

"The bullet that had hit me in the hip had deflected up the bone and travelled up my back where it lodged in my spine. They managed to get it out and I was lucky not to be disabled for good."

John Kelly's treatment did not quite end there. A cold-blooded and rather eerie phenomenon then occurred – a phenomenon not untypical in Belfast. Having failed to shoot him dead the gang did not give up, and took to stalking the wards in search of him. There has been more than one shooting in the hospital wards and grounds, and staff are schooled in recognizing irregularities.

"They kept me in for five days. The first day was in intensive care and on the second they put me in the general ward. But I got a visit from a couple of people they didn't know, so they decided to send me to another ward. Presumably the visits were by the Provisional I.R.A. They were coming in looking for 'this fellah Kelly who's been shot' and they certainly weren't visitors of mine. The sister started to get concerned about this so they moved me to another ward. But still people came in asking for me, so eventually I was moved to the military hospital in Musgrave Park.

"I had a strange experience some time after I was discharged. I saw one of those involved in the shooting. The youngsters themselves were caught some time later. They were masked but the taxi driver wasn't, and one day while I was driving up the Grosvenor Road I saw him. I was just pulling up at the crossroads with the Falls when he drove past at the wheel of a black taxi. He stared straight at me as he drove past. I immediately went to Hastings Street Barracks and told them. They stopped the taxi in Andersonstown but he wasn't in it. There was another interesting thing, too. When I went to Connswater that night to have my photograph taken I was with another fellah who got his uniform on the same day as me. A fortnight after their assassination attempt on me he came out of his house and got into his car. The car had been booby-trapped, a bomb went off and he lost a leg – in fact he lost the other one soon after as well. Now because of that, because of those two attacks at about the same time, I can only assume they had information coming out of the R.U.C. The gang didn't interrogate me. All the time they only said one thing – and that was when they stopped me. 'You're a cop now', that's all they said. None of my friends knew I was intending to join – only my wife knew. But somehow *they* knew within a week. So obviously the information had come from the R.U.C. recruiting branch in some way or other.

"I was never really afraid at all. When I was in the flat I can't say I had any fear. I felt the presence of God very much then, and it took the place of nerves and anxiety. Then when they took me out to kill me and the gun went 'click' I thought the Lord obviously had some further work for me – which at the time was just running to the end of the road! I was nineteen and a half stone and not too fit really, but I was fit enough to run. God was always in control. I didn't say anything to the men (but obviously they weren't great conversationalists either), I mean what can you say if some fellah's going to shoot you? There's little point in saying 'Don't do it' because it's not going to do anything, so I let God take charge.

"When the court case came up I realized it was the first time I'd seen them without their masks. As it turned out I'd been into the house of one of them when he was a small child. I spoke to his mother on the day of the case, and she said the kids sort of joined the junior wing of the I.R.A. just the same as our boys join the Boys' Brigade or the Scouts. She said they're just drawn into it and it progresses from there. The lad was caught, as it happened, the day after he tried to shoot me. He shot a soldier the next day. He got nine years for shooting me and life for the soldier. He was seventeen at the time.

"Looking back on it all I know I was spared by God, and the greater purpose He had was for me to serve at the military hospital which is where I am now. Ninety per cent of our patients are terrorists from both sides. They're serving jail sentences at the time and are brought in from the prisons whenever they need medical attention. Jim Prior once described them as the most dangerous men in the world, but I can honestly say the vast majority of them treat us with great courtesy. In fact we had the young lad that shot me admitted to the hospital once. I said hello but he didn't speak. I chatted to him on his way to the theatre but I got no response. Several times I asked him if he was all right but he didn't reply. Next day he said good morning.

"If you ask me if I forgive him I'll say yes. I forgive him completely. He was forgiven the day it happened – and I don't see why I can't forgive him even though he's shown no sign of repentance. Who am I to judge? I'll leave that to God alone.

"We do try to witness to these lads when they're in hospital – usually at the unearthly hour of two in the morning when they're not sleeping. I and a Christian nurse will go along and talk to them. But ministering to them is frowned on. But, you know, I think we have their complete trust and I do see hope in situations like that. We believe they leave us knowing that we've treated them as ordinary patients, that we haven't condemned them for what they've done. We leave them in no doubt that they have to make their peace with God. They realize as soon as they come in that we're Christians and that we often behave differently from the others. We try to talk to them whereas others won't have anything to do with them. I'm very happy at the military hospital and I think I was meant to be there.

"So I do see hope where I am. And don't forget another thing in all this. The Roman Catholic family who helped me when I needed it were doing their bit for hope as well.

They were taking a terrible risk. You don't drag a man in when the Provisional I.R.A. are shooting at him. It's not a recommended hobby, you know. When the man dragged me into his kitchen his wife and the lady next door were there, along with his three children (aged eleven, seven and five). They all saw the door being broken down before the men burst in and shot me. The blood was pumping out of my shoulder and my trousers were saturated in the stuff. There was blood on the doorstep and blood on the floor, and while I was lying there these children were down on their knees praying over me. 'Please, God, do not let Mr Kelly die', I can remember their words very clearly. They knew my name because the eldest one recognized me from coming into their school. The mother was talking to me quietly and said that God would take care. When the priest arrived they told him I was a Protestant to avoid any embarrassment over the last rites. Mind you, by that time I was feeling drowsy because of the blood I'd lost. When the ambulance driver came he said we couldn't drive fast with lights and horns because it might attract their attention and they'd come after us again. So we had to drive slowly. Things have come to a pretty terrible state in Belfast if that's what can happen to an ambulance. But I put my hope in ordinary families like the one that helped me when I needed it."

*   *   *

John Kelly was shot for no other reason than that he was a member of Northern Ireland's Security forces. According to the logic of the Provisional I.R.A.'s position he was a legitimate military target, one of the inevitable casualties in time of war. The next two chapters tell the stories of two young men who once fought in that "war" on opposite sides. They are two men whose experience and ultimate rejection of violence show that in Belfast the light of hope can shine from the darkest of corners.

Billy McCurrie

Life in Belfast advances by crisis. Traumatic events in personal and political life seem, to the outsider at least, to be the only means by which the course of the city's history is governed. Billy McCurrie's own journal of trauma began in 1970 when he was twelve years old and has proceeded through a series of dramatic turning points. Now, seventeen years later, he prepares to train for the Christian ministry having spent a third of his life behind bars for murder.

"I got involved with the U.V.F. [the Ulster Volunteer Force, the outlawed "Protestant" paramilitary force and counterpart of the Provisional I.R.A.] as a result of seeing my father shot. He was shot when I was twelve, and from that moment I swore I would get revenge. It was a sectarian killing. He was walking along Albert Bridge Road to the Newtonards Road on his way to a social club. That way you have to pass through the Short Strand area, which is Catholic. Usually he took a longer route to avoid passing through – and that's what he did the day he was killed. Because he was seen walking from one Protestant area to another he was shot. A sniper fired at him with an automatic rifle. Nobody was ever caught.

"I vowed revenge when I saw what happened to my family. Virtually overnight it turned from a family united in love and happiness to one united in grief. The whole structure of the family just caved in. It used to rack me when my kid brother Jimmy asked where his dad was or why he didn't have a daddy. It used to rack me when I saw my mother, who was three months pregnant at the time, constantly breaking down.

"I went out of my way to get involved with the U.V.F. and I joined as soon as I could, at the age of sixteen. From the start I wanted to be an active member; I didn't want to go in just to sit on my backside. I joined the organization to kill. To kill Catholics, full stop. I put up all sorts of schemes – blowing up the likes of Republican bars and so on – but they were all rejected as being too horrific. I wanted guns and explosives but they were never forthcoming, and I found it frustrating not being allowed to do anything by the hierarchy. Whether it was because I was too young I'm not sure, but speaking to some of the high-ups in prison I was told that they knew my family and they knew what my mother was going through. They didn't want to send me out to have me arrested or killed and then see my mother affected more.

"But I guess I became a pain in their side because a year later I was asked to do a shooting. Ironically it was a Protestant I shot – a member of my own organization whom I'd been told was an informer. The fact that Brigade Staff [the governing body of the U.V.F.] had sent over for me was an ego trip. I wanted to prove myself. I went with another fellah (he's still inside) and together we did this shooting. The informer had to be 'given the message'. They had two phrases at the time, 'given the message' or 'sent for his tea' – i.e. killed. So if anybody said, 'Look, this guy has to go for his tea', it meant you couldn't mess around. He had to be found dead. I was given a .38 Smith & Wesson, my mate had a Luger 9 mil.

"The way it was set up was that this guy, who lived in the Shankill but worked in East Belfast, had had all his movements watched. He used to get to work about 7.30 each morning. When he drove into Manderson Street, which is a cul de sac just off the top of the Newtonards Road, we were waiting for him in a derelict house. As soon as he stopped the car to do a three-point turn we stepped out into the street and were about to shoot when we saw a couple of shipyard workers in the distance. My mate said, 'Hold on, we might be seen'. I don't know how this guy didn't see us either. It was a deserted street and he was no more than ten feet from us. Then the car started to reverse. My mate put his gun in his inside pocket and I kept mine by my side. We walked out and the car drove up alongside us, with this guy wondering where we'd suddenly come from. Both of us shot him. My mate shot first then me. It might sound callous but I let him shoot first because I wanted to see what happened. You know, you see people shot in films and everything flies all over the place. I wanted to see if that was how it really was. It didn't happen like that. I expected the glass to shatter but it didn't, the glass just went frosty. When I saw that I just fired my gun off. I fired four and my mate fired four. It was the round from the .38 which killed him. He was hit five or six times. Then we ran.

"After that I felt I'd proved myself to the paramilitaries. Perhaps now they'd give me more of a free hand. From then on I had this tremendous feeling of power. I used to be in the Army Cadets and we'd practise shooting at cardboard cutouts in the firing range. It never dawned on me what power I had in my hands at the time, but once I'd taken a life, I realized that if anybody said anything I disagreed with or if there was ever a fight, out would come 'the great equalizer' – the gun. And nobody would push you around any more. If I wanted I could pick up a gun and dispose of the problem. It's frightening that a seventeen-year-old can feel he has that power."

Two weeks after the shooting Billy was arrested. Nobody had seen the attack but someone, presumably from inside the U.V.F., had informed the police. At the interrogation the police made it clear to Billy that they knew all the details of the killing and how he and his friend had personally been involved. Billy was surprised they knew so much and felt he had no way out. He therefore admitted everything, naïvely unaware at the time that it was one thing to know what had happened and another to prove it in court. It was in court that he remembers being told by his solicitor to expect a twenty-year jail sentence, and he remembers, too, being physically sick at the prospect of spending more than his lifetime so far behind bars. At seventeen he was too young for the life sentence which his twenty-five-year-old colleague had received and so he was sentenced to be jailed indefinitely at the Secretary of State's pleasure. Billy's change of heart occurred gradually over the next five years in the Maze Prison, but began when he witnessed the illogicalities of Loyalist and Republican terrorists sharing the same space.

"At first I felt very proud to have taken up the gun for Ulster. I was put in the U.V.F. compound in the Maze, where the organization had its own command structure. We had our own sergeants and adjutants to do the administration, we had muster parades every morning where we would stand with trousers pressed and boots shining. I thought it was brilliant – the fact that my freedom had been taken away didn't mean too much. Then after a few months my eyes opened a bit.

"It used to puzzle me why I.R.A. and U.V.F. men were allowed to mix. For instance, on visiting days a bus would come round and collect first the Republicans and then the Loyalists. There wasn't much communication but I got to wondering why outside we were blowing the heads off these guys and inside we managed to co-exist. One night I brought it up with one of our men as we were walking round the compound, and I told him that if you fight a war outside you should fight it inside, too. These fellahs are Republicans and they're legitimate targets. Then he says to me, 'Look, we've talked it over together and we've agreed that the visits are neutral ground. Your family has enough to worry about without having your mother come to see you when you've got a black eye.' Now, I thought this was really crazy. He says you can't send sons into a visiting room with a black eye when outside we were sending sons home to their mothers in a coffin. It was then I realized how warped the whole situation was.

"I began to make a study of politics, thinking that a political situation needed a political answer. I became convinced that Marx had all the answers but eventually I became disillusioned with that. It seemed to me that all people are interested in is power and that didn't offer any solutions. About this time I got to know a man called Peter who had got life for driving a getaway car after a bombing. He had become a Christian in prison. When I told him I didn't believe in God and was sceptical he didn't, as many Christian prisoners often did, quote a verse from the Bible at you. Instead all he said was that it made no difference whether you were sceptical or not – there's still a God. And there's still a Hell. And he told me I was heading straight for it. 'There's many a person sceptical in life,' he said, 'and now they're believers in Hell. And it's too late.' Well, that sort of took the wind out of my sails because I wasn't expecting that. So I started to ask questions of other Christians – officers and prisoners. And every time I asked a question they took time to answer. The Christian people I asked always had time.

"By now I was becoming disillusioned with the authoritarian regime of the paramilitaries. I decided I wasn't going to play the game. Now, that's pretty dangerous because if you do that you chip away at their power and others will do the same. So then they're forced to crack down on you. I believe a couple of them wanted me dead. I wasn't too worried about getting a hiding but it's what would come of somebody sticking a chisel in your back while they were beating you up that worried me. You could be maimed for life. In the end though I succumbed to pressure to go on the blanket protest for political status in 1978. It was the lowest point I reached because it showed I couldn't stand up to these guys on my own. Then I met Peter again. He was different from me in that although he had been a member of the organizations he'd been able to stand out against them. You'd look at him and he'd be grinning from ear to ear. He had something I didn't have. Then a prison officer came up to me and said what Peter had was what I needed – Christ. I began to think he might be right.

"The protest ended two weeks before Christmas and I was very depressed. The wee communist house I'd been building on sand had collapsed and I had nothing to rely on. On Christmas Eve 1980 a woman called Gladys Blackburn came round distributing religious tracts. She was like a wee granny – she was five foot high, had a bad chest and sat on the Board of Visitors. And any time you saw Gladys coming with her bag of tracts you ran, because if she cornered you you got the Gospel preached at you. She came down to my cell that night and, right enough, out came the Bible and she read me the story of the Crucifixion. And at that point I came under the deep conviction of my own sin.

"The thief on the cross is calling Christ 'Lord' and in my life I'd hated and murdered and now I was calling Him 'Lord'. Nobody had ever really taught me that here on the cross was God and He was dying for me.

"So I asked her how you become a Christian, and she said that it was easy – just a matter of ABC. *Accept* that Christ died for you. *Believe* what the Bible says about Him and *confess* it to others. Now A and B – that was pretty easy. But as for *confessing* it to others, well, that was another matter. I knew the abuse Christians came in for in prison, because I'd given plenty of it out myself. After Gladys had left I got on my knees and prayed.

"The next morning I went into the canteen and told my mate what had happened and that I'd become a Christian. I couldn't repeat the abuse he came out with. It took him a good five minutes to say his piece and it was far from good-humoured. He was angry and told me at great length that I was a phoney. Once you become a Christian in prison people think you're just wanting to work your ticket and have an easy time of it. In fact I didn't find that at all. In many ways time was harder to bear because you were constantly under the microscope and you didn't dare to put a foot wrong. They'd all be there ready to call you a phoney so you had to be consistent. My reply was simply, 'Watch! If this thing isn't sincere it'll fall through'."

So far Billy's Christian faith has not fallen through. It was after five years in prison that his conversion took place. Four and a half years after that he was released. He admits that less than ten years in jail may seem a short sentence for taking a life, but he feels that his release was justified in the light of his change of heart and mind.

"I did think of getting in touch with the family but generally that isn't encouraged. Anyway, what could I say — I'm sorry? I mean, I am truly sorry for what I did but the English language can't express what I feel. I know what that guy's family has gone through — it happened to me. I can only help matters by my example — by what I do. I sound a warning note against getting involved with the paramilitaries and being influenced by rabble-rousing politicians. Some of them come up to me and say I've no right to be saying that sort of thing. But all I'm saying is, the answer is not the bomb and the bullet but the person of Christ. Mind you, it's easy to point the finger at guys like me and say they're the reason for it all so leave them in jail. But I think the politicians have a responsibility for it too. They made the bullets and we fired them. I made a mistake and I hope, through what I've learned from my mistakes, I can warn youngsters of the pit that lies before them. That's part of what I hope to be doing when I've finished my training for the ministry at the Irish Baptist College.

"I was allowed to turn the disadvantage of prison to

advantage and for me that is a hopeful sign. But it's not me who's getting through, it's the Gospel. I know a lot of people who think Christianity is some kind of crutch only for the feeble-minded, but I have seen people changed by it – hard men changed by the example of others in imitation of Christ. I saw the cycle of violence I had created myself and it was only the Gospel which could break it."

There is an illuminating postscript to Billy's story and one which illustrates the extremes of life between which Belfast constantly swings. It is the story of Billy's mother – as susceptible to the virus of hatred as she was to the contagion of love.

"I was numbed after my husband's death. I'd chummed up with Catholics before but when my husband was shot I cut myself off from them completely. All I felt was a deep, deep hatred for all Catholics. I wanted nothing to do with them, I didn't want to live in the same street as them. I used to go to a Catholic hairdresser once a week, but after the death I couldn't even bear to mention her name. She sent word she wanted to see me but I couldn't bear it. When I saw Roman Catholics on TV I could have opened that set and torn them out. Anyone who'd known me before knew that wasn't like me at all, but I let this bitterness rule my life for eleven years until I came to the Lord and He dispersed it. It was a hard ball of hatred embedded deep within me. When Billy got saved he'd write me lovely wee letters about God saving us all. I'd smile and say I was happy for him, but nobody could take away the hate and bitterness, the roots went too deep. But when people start praying the Holy Spirit starts working. When Christ lifted that heavy burden from my shoulders I felt as light as air. The only sadness I have is that others are going through the things I went through. We have all worked together and lived together before – I pray we will again."

Gerry Burns

At the age of thirty-five Gerry Burns has spent over a third of his life in jail. For armed robbery, planting a bomb in a petrol tanker and for being a member of the I.R.A., in which he once passionately believed, he did thirteen years in the Maze Prison. It was there that he, like Billy McCurrie, experienced a profound change of heart, but whereas Billy's transformation was achieved quite suddenly (though not without hardship) Gerry's struggle towards faith was long and arduous – a struggle born of experience of life *in extremis*, unknown by all but a hand-ful of his contemporaries. For good or ill the "blanket protest" changed a few men's lives. Ten men died on it, some were embittered by it. Gerry transcended it. His eyes tell some of the story. When he smiles it is a child's smile – open, vulnerable and bright. When his face is at rest his eyes tell a different tale – of anger and pain, sadness and suffering and, most of all, of self-knowledge and of a wisdom beyond his years that spring directly from that formative time "on the blanket".

The blanket protest began in the H blocks of the Maze Prison (so called because viewed from the air each of the eight prison buildings formed the letter H, containing two hundred prisoners per letter). It began as an attempt to force the British Government into granting "special category status" to those found guilty of terrorist crimes. Such status had recently been withdrawn, so denying the I.R.A. and U.V.F. the title of "political" prisoners which served to elevate them above the rank of common criminal. The blanket protest is an odd phrase – part touching, part shocking, and a strangely naïve euphemism to describe a campaign which is now part of the political and folk history of Belfast. During the blanket protest prisoners refused, among other things, to wear prison clothes (special category men could wear their own) and dressed themselves only in the prison blanket they were provided with in their cell. The protest attracted both Loyalist and Republican prisoners in the early days, but it was later seen as a predominantly Republican stand taken by I.R.A. men like Gerry Burns. The blanket protest escalated into the "dirty" protest, when men refused to wash, shave and carry out the basic formalities of personal hygiene, smearing their own excrement on the walls of their cells. In such conditions – covered only by a rough blanket and amid conditions of barely imaginable squalor, stench and degradation – did men like Gerry live for years on end. These two protests culminated in the Hunger Strike when Bobby Sands became the first of ten Republican prisoners to fast to death. The significance of these momentous events is disputed. By some they are viewed as expiation for all the crimes of violence the I.R.A. had committed, as a dignified, tragic justification for more killing to come. To others they were nothing more than futile, dehumanizing exercises in self-publicity – a clever but bogus way of giving a pseudo-romantic legitimacy to a criminal organization. One thing, however, is certain – that the three protests – whether sacrificial atonement or crude propaganda – stamped a lasting mark on the men involved. By the time of the Hunger Strikes Gerry Burns had turned his back on the I.R.A., and at great personal cost was starting afresh, but by that time, too, he had taken part in the two other protests which are etched indelibly on his mind and which, he recognizes, changed the course of his life.

"I think the blanket protest was the most important time of my life, because although I'd been in prison for five years before that up until that point I still hadn't been deprived of many things. Although being in the compounds didn't provide you with as many things as you had outside you still had books, and TV and sport and things. When I went on the blanket I had nothing. There in your cell, alone with just a blanket round you, you had nothing to do but think and read the Bible. And because of the situation you were in you prayed. You know, you got to the point where you said, 'How am I going to put up with this?' And if you had any sort of Christian family background you prayed to God.

"That background had always been there since childhood though I'd never developed it. My mother had had a hard time from my father, and I'd seen her dependence on God. If she'd had a row, say, she'd run out of the house and I, as a kid, always knew where to find her. I'd go up to the chapel and there she'd be. My brothers and sisters (nine of them altogether) always knew she'd have run off to the chapel, so that was always at the back of my head. It sort of programmed a religious background in you.

"During the first five years I was in jail I didn't turn to God the way I did on the blanket. I never really felt this need for strength to get me through my time (although even in the cages you felt under a lot of pressure). But on the blanket you got the opportunity to look at yourself truly. In many of the cells there was one person locked up alone. For example, I was on my own for six months. You couldn't see anybody else – you could just hear the voices. You could tell people's characters from the way they spoke through the doors. If you want to be dramatic about it you could say they were like spirits. You see, it wasn't just a guy's voice you were hearing – after a while it was his whole character coming out. Someone would speak nice and calmly, and another would be aggressive and you'd have a picture in your mind's eye of what they were like. It was very strange, very weird at times – in a way you began to lose touch with reality, or let's say the spirit voices *were* your reality.

38

"I was on the protest for two and a half years – it may seem like a long time, but there were guys there who'd been on it for five years. At first, if somebody told me that someone had been on the blanket for a year I'd have found it hard to believe. How could they stay like that for a year? But then when you personally go on it and you do a year, then another year doesn't seem to matter, and the longer you're on it the less the outside world is a reality to you. Being on the protest in your cell is the reality and it's more important to you to behave in the accepted way on the blanket than to behave in the accepted way in the outside world, which in any case is becoming fuzzier and fuzzier. Someone coming off the street and into prison realizes what he's missing – the freedom to get into a car and go for a drive, or the freedom to walk at night. Whereas when you've been in prison a long time all those things cease to mean anything to you and, especially on the blanket, you have nothing but yourself and a Bible.

"But the experience could, I think, send you one of two ways. Either you could become bitter and lose part of yourself or you could be strengthened by it, survive, and come out whole. The reason why I came off the protest after so long on it was that I saw what it was doing to me, how bitter it was making me, and I began to realize that if I didn't stop this procedure it was going to twist me up inside and drive me nuts with hatred and anger. It's not that there was this time all of a sudden when I thought I'd had enough, it was a case of just saying to myself, 'My God, I shouldn't be this angry at anything. This bitterness is wrong and it's going to do me harm.' It was through reading the Bible and thinking that I began to see that the inability to forgive people's wrongs only does *you* harm. It's not a question of saying 'let bygones be bygones' – it's not as if you're letting those people get away with any-thing. It's for your own benefit to call a halt to the hatred. Through reading the Bible I began to believe that holding a grudge does nobody any damage but yourself and the people who love you.

"The grudge I was holding was against the British, against the British soldiers, against the R.U.C., against society generally, because I felt it was unfair to the likes of under-privileged people. I didn't want to be in prison – all I wanted was to go out with my girlfriend and have a good time. But being in a Catholic ghetto, the Ardoyne, meant being pressurized into certain situations. To an extent I was to blame myself, but to an extent I also believe I was pushed into doing what I was doing and joining the I.R.A. Time and time again I was pulled in by the British Army, lifted off the streets, beaten up and accused of being in the I.R.A. – this was at a time when I wasn't involved at all.

"One time a bomb had gone off in our district. I didn't know a thing about it. At the time I was about nineteen or twenty and was working at the bricklaying. I'd gone to bed early and hadn't even heard the bomb go off. I was lying there at about ten or eleven o'clock when I was woken by a British soldier standing by the bed prodding me with a rifle. They took me out of the house, and you could see soldiers at every door in the street; they'd swamped the place. They kept me in the barracks for three days, questioned me, slapped me around a bit and threw me out. Then as I was coming out of the barracks there was a Land-Rover waiting, and the police picked me up again and took me to Tennent Street Police Station. When they brought me into the room for interrogation somebody put the light out and threw the table up in the air. They put me against a wall and started punching me. Then they threw me on the floor and started jumping on my head and stuff like that – asking me all the time who'd done the bomb. I didn't know. It was things like that which embittered you.

"You couldn't walk out of the house without getting stopped by a foot patrol and slapped about or humiliated. Things like that pressurized us guys into going against the authorities. It wasn't as if I was politically aware or anything and made a rational decision to do it. Before 1969 the I.R.A. was like Dad's Army or something – if you were on the estate and in the I.R.A. it was very odd. But seeing the way the police behaved, and seeing Catholic families burned out of their homes, made you feel you had to join it. And then after Bloody Sunday [when thirteen civilians were shot dead by the British Army in 1972] you felt all this had purpose – all of a sudden you had a cause to fight for.

"I would say I was just pushed into it – I had no alternative but to join the I.R.A. Now, I know the police have learnt a lot from their mistakes in the early days. They've realized a lot of their tactics were counter-productive, but that can't alter the past. It can't change the fact that they ruined my life and stacks of other guys' lives. There are guys doing life now for the same reasons as me – they were pushed into it. But once I did join the I.R.A. I felt I was justified. There was always a warning with any bombs I did. You can't be a hundred per cent sure, but I think I can safely say that there's no way I could have planted a bomb somewhere to try to kill innocent people. I was aware of the bomb going off prematurely and doing that, but I was prepared to take a personal risk as well. I didn't plant them in a cowardly way where there'd be no danger to me. I believed it was a terrible situation but I saw justification in doing what I did. But now after coming closer to God and getting a better understanding of myself and of what's right and wrong, I see that no matter what the reasons and the causes are there can be no justification for killing. But having said that I believe it's still just as immoral to be in the British Army as in the Irish Republican Army.

"My belief in the Nationalist cause was enough to help me to put up with life on the blanket and then on the dirty protest. It's not a physical thing, it's mental. If you get your mind right you can bear it. There were guys doing thousands of push-ups a day in their cells or running on the spot for hours. You'd be given three basic meals a day, say, a couple of potatoes, some meat and a sweet for one meal, and for breakfast two slices of bread and tea. The difference was that in one block you were getting fed in a civilized way and in the other you weren't. You were getting your meal put on the floor, kicked through the door caked with excrement and when the door was slammed it would all fall off the door and into the food so that guys couldn't eat it. The protest was also driving the screws crazy. They had to work in all this filth and stench. It wasn't really designed towards them, though. It was more a political thing. Everybody wanted to see some hope in something because you wanted the protest to end as soon as possible – it wasn't pleasant! You knew that the only way you could gain any ground was by forcing the Government to do something; by embarrassing them into doing something and giving way. Little did I know at the time that we were forcing them into being unable to give anything. The harder we were the more they dug their heels in. The guys in the I.R.A. didn't respect the establishment in the Catholic Church much either. They were considered pro-British so their attempts at mediations didn't come to anything.

"There was a lot of social pressure on us to join the protest, just as if a war broke out in England people would feel a sort of pressure to join up. But even though I backed the cause it was hard. From day one I had to grit my teeth and pray for the strength just to stay there – not to ask a screw to let me out so I could run away. You'd be locked in a cell eight foot by nine foot, with the prospect of staying there for God knows how long. With the shouting and the noise you had to concentrate to block it all out. It wore me down and I had to pray to cut it all out. There were some wings where they prayed the rosary out loud. But my prayers were personal, between me and God. What I prayed for at the start was the strength to remain faithful to my friends here on the blanket – not to let them down. I asked for strength to face the screws without fear, without letting them humiliate me or beat me up. I also prayed for protection – that I wouldn't be seriously injured in any beating. I prayed, too, for understanding. You know, for the means to discover who's right in this situation. Are we right or are we wrong? And through this praying I realized that I'd been putting up a front all my life. My personality to ordinary people I met every day wasn't the same as this personality I was taking to God when I asked Him for things. Eventually I got to the situation where I had to stop behaving the way I was. Either I had to change the way I thought and acted with other people, or I had to stop going to God and praying. I couldn't have these two per-sonalities.

"The realization came to me from reading the Bible, that sincerity is one of the things God requires, along with honesty, faithfulness, and courage. I was beginning to see I didn't have any courage. I was asking for courage to face the screws and the protest, and I hadn't the courage to face my friends with the same attitude I had when I was talking to God. I began to realize I hadn't the courage to stand up at Mass and say to the guys, 'Stop talking while the priest's doing the Mass here!' I began to see I hadn't the guts to stand up and be faithful to Jesus Christ. I was just acting like a coward, afraid that people would say I'd flipped or become a Jesus freak. When I did start taking the faith seriously some of them thought I'd stopped becoming a Catholic. Mind you, some of them had been through the same thoughts themselves and could recognize the change in me. There were guys who could appreciate it, and others who didn't understand and who passed all sorts of false judgements on you. I knew some guys would consider me sick and others a coward, but I knew that the guys I really respected would accept it for what it was. I think it was harder coming off the protest than it was going on it, especially when you'd been on it for so long like me. You knew the screws really gloated over it and made comments to rub it in. When they said they'd beaten me I just said I'd come off the protest for personal reasons and said I didn't want to talk about it. The one thing being on the blanket did teach me was to know myself. If I said I was doing something for a certain reason I knew then if I was being honest or not, whereas before the protest I'd have done things for other people's reasons and not have known it. But the hardest part was breaking faith with the cause and with my friends. I couldn't condemn those guys even though by this time I saw things differently from them.

"The likes of those fellahs were prepared to give everything – completely everything – for this war with the British. There's nobody else in this society that I can see prepared to do that – to be that dedicated to putting society right. I mean, when you went to Mass on Sunday and you saw some of these guys shuffling in, bleached white, with long hair and beards, guys who hadn't washed for years walking in in their bare feet wearing old rags, you couldn't help but be moved. There's something holy about it. I mean, young kids of eighteen shaking all over with six-foot-six screws hovering over them. It's moving. These guys were prepared to suffer.

"I was in the cells one night and these screws came along the landing punching everybody in every cell. They went all the way up one side and down the other. I was in the last cell with this wee guy – he was about nineteen or twenty and he was dead, dead thin. He had long black hair and he looked like a girl really. He couldn't grow a beard, he just had a few hairs growing out here and there. And the kid was trembling. We could hear everybody getting beaten up all the way up and down – you heard big whacks, you know, as their heads hit the wall. Now I knew the screws

44

were scared of me because I'd hit a few of them before, so I wasn't trembling. But this wee guy — the courage it must have taken him to stay on the protest for those years. It's hard to believe and you can't help but admire them.

"So coming off the protest was hard. It was a kind of death. I had to choose one or other of my personalities and the other one had to die. The two couldn't go together. Either I had this dependence on God or I still remained part of an organization that justified killing people the way the I.R.A. did. OK, it might have been U.D.R. men or British soldiers, but I couldn't see any justification for killing. When I read the Bible it was all right with the Old Testament, with the fighting and the battles — then you could justify things — but when I got to the New Testament I realized I couldn't be involved in killing. I couldn't think Jesus would justify leaving some woman with a dead husband or a dead son. I got to the point where I felt God was saying — no, it wasn't even like that — He wasn't saying anything, just leaving it to me to see you couldn't do two things. The British claimed to be doing things for justice and yet they were committing terrible injustices; and yet, I realized then, the I.R.A. were doing just the same.

"The way things are in Belfast is just as God said they'd be. It's not a question of the troubles coming to an end — though I don't think they'll ever come to an end until the British Army's gone. That isn't what Christianity is all about. There'll be wars and rumours of wars and injustices and that will never change — that's the way the world is, unfortunately. The plan is to live as a Christian, and the kingdom of God will be in the midst of you even though there's injustice and violence all around you."

*

It is often said — and it is a matter for some resentment to those who live uneventful lives far from the extremes of existence – that the greatest sinners make the greatest saints. Whether Gerry Burns turns out to be a saint remains to be seen. I suspect he would be the first to doubt it, but certainly it is not too fanciful to say that the ascetic life he knew on the blanket could find its place in the annals of any contemporary hagiology. But there will still be many who feel that a hardened criminal's conversion to Christ is not enough to paint a picture of hope in Belfast. It may be all right for the Gerry Burnses and the Billy McCurries of the city to talk about salvation and goodness, but it is actions by people like them (albeit in their former in-carnations) which destroy the lives of innocent men and women. What hope is there for the victims of the cruelty? "Go to the victim's family," the critics will say, "and show me hope there."

For this next story I have done that. It is the story of forgiveness against all the odds, of a family setting its heart against hatred at the most testing of times.

But a final word to the sceptics before we leave Gerry Burns. What he has to say does offer comfort and hope. His story was not told glibly and smoothly like well-rehearsed paragraphs of a practised speech. When he spoke to me for the first time at length since his release he spoke slowly and deliberately. It was as if it were the fruits of thirteen years of struggle to find the right words – the doleful eloquence of a hard man won over by love.

Pearl McKeown

We read the phrase "sectarian killing" – like so much that happens in Belfast – with little understanding of the cruelty behind it. It is hardly surprising because the facts are barely imaginable in a "civilized" world. A victim is selected at random and then assassinated. It could be a drunk unsteadily making his way home up the Falls Road at night, it could be a man on his way to work in East Belfast one Monday morning, or it could, as here, be a twenty-year-old girl, a student at Queen's University, shot as she stood outside the church where she had been singing in the choir.

The logic of the sectarian attack is simple. A Protestant has been shot one day, so a Catholic – any Catholic – will be shot the next. The reverse holds true and so it was that at 8.30 on the evening of the 25th of September 1982 Karen McKeown became the Protestant selected by a Republican paramilitary gunman as the target for violence and reprisal. The words "Catholic" and "Protestant" are inadequate, of course, to make sense of the affiliations that drive men to kill, and Karen's mother, Pearl, is not the only one to reject the crude shorthand of Christian denomination as any justification for the murderous divisions in Belfast.

"I detest the word 'Protestant' really. We're not Protestants – we're Christians. It was a Christian church Karen was coming out of that night, not a 'Protestant' church. We'd been having an inauguration for our new minister on the night Karen was shot and she'd been singing at it. I'd been down there making supper for everyone and we'd all stayed behind to wash the dishes afterwards. As I had an early duty at the hospital the next day, and was feeling rather tired, Karen said she would run me home. After that she drove back to finish clearing up. She got out of the car outside the church and as she bent down to lock the driver's door a man came up to her and said, 'I want you to know that I'm going to shoot you'. Then he put a gun to her neck and fired, and left her lying on the ground in the rain, completely and utterly paralysed.

"Karen was alive for three weeks after the shooting. She was put in intensive care and she never lost consciousness until the very end – about three days before she died. And to me the Lord allowed us two and a half beautiful weeks. We talked about so many things – well, when I say talk, she had a tube in her throat and if you pressed a button you could make her voice come out. But that distressed her so we didn't use it. Instead she mouthed everything to us and we had no difficulty making her out. We were never once given a glimmer of hope that she would survive. They told her the situation too, and she knew full well what to expect. When the bullet went through it severed the spine completely, which meant she had to be put on a life-support machine. The motor which worked her lungs would never function of its own accord, she would always be on a catheter and always connected to one of these machines. Dr Gray [the anaesthetist at the intensive care unit] said she would only ever be able to move her head – she couldn't even scratch her nose – and that meningitis would eventually set in and kill her, which is exactly what happened. It could have gone on for months and years, which I wouldn't have liked because she would have ended up with bedsores.

"She was a very physically active person – her father used to say she didn't know what the seat in her rear end was for – so I would have hated to see it all drag on and her have to go through all that. She was always doing something. She was a lovely dancer. She was a Sunday School teacher, she was studying for a BSc at Queen's, and wanted to be a social worker. Mind you, she loved children that much she'd have had all the waifs and strays living at home with her! She did have one fault, though. When you put her behind the wheel of her wee Ford Fiesta she sprouted horns and drove like a madman. It wasn't like her at all. The car just changed her. You know the way some men change when you give them a hat – it was just like that! Well, what with all that life in her I wouldn't have liked to see her sort of fading away for months on an intensive care machine. She was a lovely girl and a beautiful disciple of the Lord. She could melt people's hearts. When she was close to death she talked about going to Heaven as being given a blank cheque for a trip round the world. She talked about seeing Moses and walking with Peter, talking to Paul and looking at Christ. She could break your heart.

"I suppose it took me a bit of time to work out why the Lord had allowed my daughter to die, but I did in the end. The man who shot Karen had the choice of going with the Lord or going with the Devil, and he decided that there was this point of no return when he had that gun in his hand pointed at her. It's all down to free will, we're not robots. The Lord gave him that choice and he decided to run with the Devil. They did suspect a man of the shooting and had him in for interrogation twice, but there was insufficient evidence to prove anything so they let him go. The only proof they had was that the gun that shot Karen outside the church had been used previously to shoot a councillor. But strangely enough that part of the story is of no interest to me at all. We haven't followed that up – it doesn't concern us. Whenever I think of the man that did it I always try to think of Karen's reaction to him. I remember her saying to me one day – the only day I was ever with her on my own – that he had told her he was going to shoot her. She said that when he told her she didn't really take it in, she started to laugh, thinking it was one of the boys from the church. And she was still laughing when she hit the ground. To her that was the Lord not allowing her to be frightened. She said she was sorry for *him* that he had done it. And that's the attitude I try to keep – if Karen could find it in herself to forgive, so should I. She said to me, 'If you think you have troubles, just go home and think about *his* mother and the troubles she must have.' Well, if that's the way she could look at it who am I to say different?"

Pearl's husband, John, however, has a moment's hesitation. "The man who killed Karen just fired one shot and he knew where to shoot to do the most damage. That's the one shadow that hangs over all this for me. If you're going to kill someone you shoot at the head or the heart not at the neck. This fellah shot to maim, to do the most harm he could to Karen. That's the only worrying thing in my mind – otherwise this fellah means nothing at all to me. It was a deliberate action on his part and he knew full well what he was about. He's going to have to face that in this life and before God." Despite John's one reservation about the motives of his daughter's killer, both he and Pearl admit that it was, in part at least, as a result of the three weeks spent with Karen before she died that John, like Pearl much earlier, came to a full acceptance of the Christian faith. Pearl herself remembers an important incident in those weeks.

"As Karen lay there in intensive care John went up to her and told her he was a Christian now. I wasn't completely convinced. I felt it was partly to please Karen and partly out of love and desperation to make some sort of a bargain. I felt what he was really saying was, 'If you give me back my Karen, Lord, I'll give you my soul.' But as it turned out he had had a change of heart and committed himself to the Lord. He used to go out fishing of a Sunday and throw his tackle down when he came in. He wasn't a

Christian at the time, and when he set foot through the door he'd say, 'Look, I know you're all praying for me but can't you give me a minute's peace?'" At this John smiles but agrees she's right.

"I'd be enjoying the fishing," he says, "but after a couple of hours I'd start to get a bit niggled. 'Look, Lord,' I'd say, 'I'm not doing anybody any harm, just leave me in peace a bit.'"

Pearl suspected why he was uneasy, "There were people in the church praying for him, and when I told them he was weakening they'd say, 'Hallelujah! We'll up the ante.' And they'd pray all the harder. But at the time of the shooting John had reached the bottom rung."

"It was worse than that", he says. "By that time I'd fallen right off the ladder. I'd no more fight left in me. I simply said, 'I can't think straight any more, I'm not rebelling any more. Lord, here I am'.

"But even if I'd never believed in Christ I'd have seen Him there every day in that ward of Karen's. She said Christ's arms were around her all the time, and it was Christ alone that took all the hatred from us."

"That's true", says Pearl. "Even the detective who dealt with the case said of all the cases he'd ever come across he'd never come across such a wall of love as this. It was through talking to her and her friends that he felt this love. The detective said so. There was no hatred there at all. You know when you see the obituaries – "murdered by the I.R.A." or something – well there was none of that. That sort of enmity was never mentioned. If the person that killed Karen expected to turn Catholic and Protestant against one another – which I believe was his intention – he never got the victory. We had Catholic friends who came to see us and couldn't do enough. Looking back on it all it was just Christ allowing us the privilege of two and a half weeks of Karen teaching us His compassion and filling us with it. I have talked to other mothers whose daughters have been involved in bombings and were blown to smithereens and never got to saying goodbye. I don't know how I would have reacted in that situation. I consider it a privilege that the Lord allowed us that time together. But sometimes I do go through awful bad periods. John will tell you – he gets the brunt of them! I was nursing a ninety-nine year-old the other morning in the hospital. She's psycho-geriatric and doubly incontinent. She doesn't even know what planet she's on, but she's so healthy you can't believe it. Now where's the sense in that? That she soldiers on while Karen, who was so physically active, died?

"Karen's influence in those weeks was tremendous. For instance, we'd heard about this fellah who'd been seen at her grave a few times and nobody knew him. Now, I've tried very hard to go up there but it's a thing I can't do. Anyway, I tried again the Christmas Eve before last and I looked over to where I knew the stone was and there was this fellah laying a wreath and getting rid of the old ones. I waited until he came up, and when I asked him if he'd been up to Karen's headstone he said he had, and then asked me if I minded. Well, it turned out that he'd been the head radiologist at the R.V.H. and he'd been the one to do Karen's X-rays when she'd been admitted to hospital. Now, he hadn't met her before then but he told me he'd been so impressed by her and by what she said that he'd started to read the Bible and think more deeply about religion. It turned out that it was the third year he'd been to lay a wreath. He's about twenty-nine and he told me she'd changed his life. Now, I think it's a beautiful thing that a complete stranger can feel moved to go up to her gravestone to lay a wreath like that. I've never been able to do it. She isn't dead as far as I'm concerned – she's working for her Maker far harder today than she was when she was down here. I can see evidence of it."

It was while Karen lay in hospital that Pearl also had evidence of the impact her daughter's Christian faith was having on people around her. As a result she decided to join Belfast's Prison Christian Fellowship, an organization which exists to further reconciliation in the city by showing that hardened men of violence from both religious communities can renounce their old ways and so offer hope of a lasting peace.

"I had intended to get involved for a long time but did nothing. Like so many others I only did something when a personal tragedy forced me into action. While Karen was in intensive care I received a letter from Liam McCloskey, who'd been in one of the Republican paramilitary organizations, but in jail he'd become a Christian. He wrote to say that he and another five ex-I.R.A. men had been praying for Karen, so I wrote back and sent a photograph. Strange as it may seem, the fact that this fellah from the like of that organization had become a Christian was a plus for me – I didn't find it hard to accept at all. In fact, I was very grateful for it and it showed me that there's nothing the Lord can't achieve. Liam had been one of the most passionate supporters of the Republican cause, he'd been fifty-five days on hunger strike, his eyesight was weakening and he became partially paralysed. But then in his cell he opened up a Bible 'on spec' – playing what some of his friends called 'Bible Bingo' – and read the words, 'In the prime of life must I go through death and be robbed of the rest of my years'. Now, to him that was the Lord speaking to him, and he abandoned his hunger protest to serve Christ. He put down the gun and picked up the Bible. His story's well known by now, and he's become a stalwart of the Prison Christian Fellowship.

"Whenever we in the Fellowship go on a lecture or a speaking tour there's always three of us on the platform. One Catholic, one Protestant, and someone who's been bereaved. That way we can tell people about the suffering – and the hope – from three different sides. So to me and my husband, Liam's story and his prayers were of great comfort. Before that I might have thought that the likes of Liam were all my enemies – now I see otherwise. Belfast is a wounded city and there's no hope for it whatsoever until people can face their enemies, overcome their fear and realize that they have nothing to fear but fear itself. You have to confront that fear whatever it is and allow Christ to triumph over it through you.

"You plant seeds of hope and forgiveness and you just pray things will change. I remember a meeting of the Prison Christian Fellowship we had in Enniskillen. Someone was addressing the audience and quoting a text along the lines of 'If he hungers feed him', and this woman stands up and shouts, 'If you think for one minute I'm going to forgive them you've another think coming'. So I went up to her after the meeting and said, 'You know, the Devil doesn't need to go out and do his work when he's got you to do it for him'. Well, that sort of hit home a bit – and when it comes from someone who has lost a loved one people often listen.

"There was another time we were organizing a do for a Prison Fellowship meeting and we'd all brought a few fancy cakes. One of the ladies in a church we're very close to – a very devout professing Christian – said, 'There's my tray of cakes, Mrs McKeown, you can have them provided you promise me faithfully that no Catholic prisoners will be eating off that tray.' So I said, 'Well, if that's the way you think about it, stuff it. . . !' We're not the best of friends just at the minute! To me they're missing out on so much by not having the joy of meeting these people. When people ask me why I'm associating with these criminals when they should be hung, drawn and quartered, I just say that whatever I feed into the Fellowship the Lord gives me back twice over. I've met some of these boys who've made me ashamed to say I'm a Christian – they've made me feel that my light wasn't only out, it had never even been lit."

At this point I wondered if Pearl were not being unduly

harsh on herself. Fifty-five days on hunger strike is clearly suffering of a high order. But were some of these young men not also responsible for causing great suffering to others?

"I think everybody's tragedy is the same. People will come up to me and say their tragedy is not as bad as mine. People have said things like that to me when their son has been drowned at the age of eight, for example. Well, their tragedy is every bit as bad as mine – at least I can say we had Karen for twenty years and saw God's work in her. We all approach our tragedy from a different angle. Take Leslie, for example, Karen's brother. They were very close and when Karen died his first daughter, Rebekah, was born. Now, I find that hard to cope with because we were telling Karen that we'd bring the baby round to see her – she had a bit of money left and wanted to buy some broderie anglaise for the baby. But she didn't in the end. It must have been so terrible for Leslie – to go down one ward to find your daughter being born and to go down another to see your sister die. So a tragedy like this affects us all in different ways. In fact I can't talk for too long about it.

"I don't understand it all and there's a lot of pieces missing from the puzzle. But if I needed proof that Christ is alive then I only have to look at what He's done through Karen. In the past I sat on the fence and paid superstitious lip-service, but now I know that God is in control and that in the end the jigsaw will be complete."

Working at Hope

Eric Lennon

"When history reviews this century 1950–1975 will go down as the period when the Church lost contact with the people. When there was a lot of overtime about and you got your little car and your continental holiday – that period of affluence when the Church, instead of standing out like a beacon and saying 'Love those things but don't think they'll bring you peace and happiness', grabbed a piece of the action itself and lost touch. And when the troubles came and the depression arrived the Church was cut off from people. This church was no exception."

"This church" is the Shankill Road Mission – a nineteenth-century Presbyterian gospel hall and chapel. Its dark red weatherbeaten brick and blackened stone form a strange contrast with the breezy leisure centre next door. Standing halfway up the Shankill Road, where the shops peter out into waste ground and the new redeveloped terraced housing begins, the Mission now aims to provide that beacon of hope which Eric Lennon feels is all but extinguished. When Eric talks of the church "grabbing a piece of the action" what he means is that process of gradual withdrawal from the run-down city centre areas like the Shankill to the more prosperous housing a few miles out.

"It's been counted up that there are over thirty mission halls and churches in the Shankill, but not the men and women prepared to fill them. I had to go round with prayer letters recently for the main churches, and in all of them put together there are a couple of hundred people worshipping. But this place here above will hold over eighteen hundred: the capacity of the Presbyterian church just down the road is fourteen hundred, and the one further up can hold twelve hundred – so you can see the Church has lost out. People began to believe they were in control of their own destiny. At that time there was little private housing round here, but then gradually people began to think about buying a house and moving to the outskirts – and the Christians were no exception. This place used to be a centre where people came every night for fellowship. They came here because they had nothing else – now they have television. The task we face now on the Shankill is to re-establish the Church's presence, and the only way we'll do that is when we, the Christians, realize how materialistic and selfish we've been in the past, and start identifying with the problems these people have. Then we might get some sort of revival. But it's a slow job because the problems round here are massive – there's unemployment, debt, drink and the threat of violence. These people, who have already suffered unemployment and all the pressures it brings, are stuck in concrete boxes by the planners and sedated by the D.H.S.S. – mind you, they do a good job of sedating themselves with booze as well! So it's a very slow job. From a church point of view it's like looking at world hunger and saying, 'What can I possibly do? What would my fiver do for the problem?' But in the end you simply have to do your bit where you are."

Eric is a broad, hearty father-figure of a man, as ready to melt into laugher as he is to magnetize you with seriousness when the mood of the moment switches. A born entrepreneur, a natural organizer and a shrewd administrator he was, five years ago, the moving force behind the day-centre at the Mission. "There are thirty-five thousand people living on the Shankill," he says, "and ninety per cent of them wouldn't dream of coming through the front door of the church. So we opened up a side door leading to this day-centre, and as far as the people here are concerned they aren't in a church."

But they are, and it is here that Eric has found a base for his own particular kind of ministry. There is no doubt that his easy-going nature makes him an approachable figure among young people who would not normally have anything to do with the Church. Equally, there is no doubting the energy and dedication fuelling Eric's work on the Shankill. For him it is a mixture of the Christian Gospel and an active social concern. But just as important to his success is his own experience of difficult times in Belfast, which has enabled him to identify with hardship when he sees it around him.

For years he was a successful technical representative covering the whole of Britain, until the first of a series of personal crises changed the course of his life. He was jailed for embezzling from his firm. After serving a year behind bars he began to build up his own sheet metal engineering business, starting with one thousand pounds and a tiny workshop in a shed at the back of his house, and within six months eventually running an operation with a turnover of a quarter of a million pounds. In 1974 his brother-in-law was shot by Protestants in a case of mistaken identity and Eric began to drink heavily, launching himself, as he puts it, on a binge that lasted two years. "I was a three bottles of Scotch a day man. I'd have my first drink at seven in the morning and then it was a drink an hour in the office." By this time Eric was making a lot of money and employing twenty workers in the business, but as alcohol began to take hold of him so he began to neglect the firm. He did not go bankrupt but a decidedly shaky business finally collapsed after he was admitted to hospital and spent ten months drying out from the drink. It was then that he took the decision to consolidate his Christian faith – although the joy of conversion was not to be relied on to pay all the bills.

"I suddenly found myself with two kids at Grammar School, a handicapped daughter, a handicapped wife, a child at primary school and forty-four pounds a week coming in. But still we'd say that was the happiest year of our lives before we started climbing back again. I had Christ in my heart and relied on Him utterly. We had nothing so we had to ask God for everything – and that was why the year was so joyful and so memorable. The cars had gone to clear off my drinking debts, so that if we wanted to go to town it cost us ten pence on the bus. I remember one day we got a bill in for ten pounds. The little red notice was waiting behind the door for me when I came downstairs in the morning. When my wife, Olive, told me I started shaking because this bill had totally slipped my mind, and ten pounds we had left for food was all the money we had. So Olive said 'We're going to pray over this then we'll go along and pay what we owe'. Now at this time nobody knew what sort of financial state we were in, because I prided myself on having told no one, not even members of the family. Anyway I went along and paid the bill, and when I came back there was a little envelope in the door. Somebody had begun to write on it but scribbled through it. I opened the envelope – and this is the only time it's ever happened – there was a ten pound note inside. Olive can confirm it. It was just one of those little nudges to let you know you're on the right way."

The right way eventually led him to the Shankill Road Mission and to a day-centre project which was small in itself but well in the mainstream of the Presbyterian tradition of social witness to the poorly off. "Our first job was to open up the centre in the hall next to the church, so that people could get a meal cheaper than they could at home. In the winter they got free heat – and each other's company besides. The needs of people in the 1920s, you know, when this place was in full bloom, were just the same. They came in for free food parcels, coal vouchers and dental treatment – if you'd have come in here on a Saturday morning then you'd have seen them pulling teeth in this very room! The National Health Service may have taken that aspect of things away, but other problems are still with us in a slightly different form. But it isn't easy getting through to the lads here. They're hard boys – all unemployed – and they'll tell you exactly what they think of you. I've been here practically every day for the past four years, and it's only now that they're beginning to accept me. We got the big lads football kit and we take them out on matches – there's the snooker and the pool here for them, but you've got to get them out, otherwise they'll go off their heads. We were accepted for a youth community programme – decorating old people's homes and so on – so that has been a way of developing jobs for those over eighteen. It all helps us take care of the material side of things, and that's vital for developing the spiritual side. Now, I know it says in the Bible, 'spread the word of God and it will not return unto him void', but I believe we don't have the warrant to stand there and preach at these boys until we've let them see the Gospel in action. With these lads here there is simply no point me going down and quoting scripture to them, saying, 'Look at me! I was this. I was that. I'm saved. I'm great.' They'd tell you to xxxx well disappear! You've got to embody it all in your own life. It means that even at the age of fifty I've got to make the effort to have a game of football with them. Two years ago I was known as 'that there so-and-so', it's 'Eric' now.

"Let me give you an example of another way I feel I'm getting through. We've got a young lad in here called 'Jacky'. Now he's a very tough fellah. The other week his youngest brother went out for a drink with his four mates in a car which wasn't insured. They rolled the car over in a crash and the four of them got out OK – or so it seemed. Jacky's young brother said he was all right but five minutes later his speech started to slur and he dropped down dead. It was a brain haemorrhage caused by the smack he'd had on the back of the neck. Well, anyway, this lad Jacky pulls me up later and said, 'You talk about your God. I can't wear that. Why did that happen to my brother? If the family's done something wrong why didn't God take my old man? He's seventy-two and ready to go. Why my brother?' You see, these fellahs all believe in a God with a big stick. Well, we had a chat and eventually he said to me, 'Mind you, that doesn't mean I don't believe in Him, because I've seen what He's done to people like you and I know you lot have got something I haven't. One of these days He's going to speak to me and then I'll be with you. And when I come I'll bring half the Shankill with me.' There was a time when there'd have been no point me going down to witness to them at all. Better to keep my mouth shut unless I could show I loved them. Well, it's taken me four years to grow to love them, because they can be tough and want nothing to do with Christianity.

"So you see, God is working through all sorts of channels but it's slow. It's not surprising either, because He's got a lot to work against round here. This is how tough it is. There's a fellah who's been coming in here for four years and he's got a drink problem, and when he gets drunk he hits his wife, who clears off and goes to live in a hostel. He finds where she is, goes after her and beats her again. Then he'll sober up, make all sorts of promises, and get her back. A couple of months back the same thing happened. He broke every window in the house and then came along here asking if we'd put the windows back. He promised everything would be all right this time, he'd knock off the booze and start afresh. During the next week I could see him keeping his promise, but getting more and more angry all the time he was having to stay dry. Not long after that he beat his wife again and she came in here crying. She cried for two hours and told me she'd decided to go for good this time. We found a safe place for her, but her husband found out where it was and in the meantime he was trying to work his ticket saying, Oh, yes, he needed Christianity, and threatening overdoses and all that to put pressure on her. Anyway, when the court ordered him not to see her he went straight to the pub, emptied half a bottle of Scotch down his throat and came here. He accused me of everything, including sleeping with his wife, and then he threatened to have me shot. He named the fellah he'd get to do it! I took him up to see his wife and she told him she didn't want any more to do with him, so he went off and drank all night. In the morning I got a phone call from him asking me to go over and see him at his house. My wife almost went into hysteria, I'm not joking, because she was sure he had somebody waiting there with a gun. Other people advised me against it, too, but I had to work it out with God. Was I prepared to go if that was the way God meant to take me? In the end I felt I had to go – mind you, my knees were knocking – and when I arrived he was in the DTs, and I spent five hours with him, eventually getting him into the psychiatric unit at the hospital.

"To get through to people you've got to speak (or act) in a way they can understand. One day this really big fellah named Tommy came in, and some of the new (rather immature) workers were witnessing to him along the lines of God planning everything. Well, that night a little kiddie had climbed on top of one of the army Saracens [one of the armoured cars] at the back gate here. He'd fallen off and was killed – squashed under the wheels. So the next morning Tommy came in and said, 'I suppose your xxxx God planned that, did He?' So one of our workers came up and said to me that Tommy would have to be disciplined for that. He'd have to be barred because he couldn't talk about God like that. But I said, 'Why not? He's an enemy of God's so why shouldn't he say anything he likes about his enemy?' And then I told the worker that we might have missed an opportunity to witness to Tommy irrespective of what had happened. We could have said that if you go up a road, see a signpost that says 'Diversion' and you ignore it, and then your car falls into a hole, you've got no right blaming the fellah that put up the signpost. Similarly, if you choose to live your life without God you can't turn around and blame God for it. But nobody ever did witness to Tommy that day, and we lost a heaven-sent opportunity to bring the spirit of Christ into his life.

"We'd a young fellah here who had a fierce temper on him, but we gave him a job on one of our work creation schemes. Many of our lads are on the edges of crime (or actively involved in it) and, to be honest, our record for helping them change their ways *outside* of Christianity is good. But this fellah wouldn't learn. He was only twenty-one but we had a hard time with him. In July this place closes down for three weeks and he got three weeks' pay. He'd never had money like that in his hand before so he went across the road to a drinking club and had a few drinks. He started to cause a bit of bother and they threw him out. He left, went and got himself a gun, emptied it into the hallway and shot four people. He didn't kill anyone but there's one girl with a bullet lodged in her spine still.

"There is hatred here. There is a lack of God. We Christians are so few and we need revival. But it's not revival to have nice, comfortable meetings with our Catholic neighbours. I think it's a wasted exercise to have little groups of good Catholics and good Protestants meeting if they're not prepared to come into these tough situations. There's a lad at the snooker table there who's just done two prison terms for U.V.F. membership, and I don't know what else besides, but he's come in here and started working with us and he's firmly on the right road now. That's the positive side of things here. There's Billy McIllwaine who was a fundraiser for the U.V.F. He did time for raising cash for bombs and guns but he got to know the Lord and turned his back on all that. That's another positive sign, too, but we've got to face facts and say that there are more of the other stories than these, and the reason for that is that we, as Christians, don't get involved. When I came here there was one member of the congregation who lived here in the area. One member! By and large we go home to the suburbs and forget the Shankill. We've got our religious groups, our Exclusive Brethren or our Charismatics, we've got our extremes fighting over doctrine all the time, but they're so busy arguing about the small points that they've no love for each other. They've certainly no love for these lads, who can go to Hell for all they care. Until there's a revival in the hearts of the Christians we won't get anywhere. You hear some of these extremes talking and you may think their politics are right, but it all comes out so hard and harsh and completely lacking in love that things must be wrong somewhere. For instance, I'd be classed as a Unionist (although I wouldn't want to think of myself as a political animal at all) but when I hear hatred spewed out by people who say they want to defend the Reformed faith I have to say that there's a contradiction. Whether Catholic, Protestant or Pagan love's what we lack. Of course it's very difficult to love somebody who tells you and your Christianity to xxxx off, but that's the tough part of the faith.

"It's love and compassion that are needed. Working round here you have to have sympathy with the people because they really are up against it, and it's no use ministering to their spiritual needs until you've attended to their physical ones. I went to deliver toys on this estate at Christmas, and I came across this thirty-eight-year-old woman sitting in her flat. Her husband had left her and she was pregnant. Her teenaged daughter was pregnant. Her son's girlfriend was there – also pregnant. There was nothing on the floor but dirt. Now how could you get through to that woman with the Good News? How could you get her mind off her troubles long enough for her to get her mind focused on Christ? Admittedly she'd only herself to blame for a lot of these problems in the first place, but that didn't lessen them any. So in those circumstances what do you do? Christianity isn't a magic wand you wave – it's a way of life which, by your own example, can help people one step at a time. I've heard people say that becoming a Christian is harder in suburbia, when you've got comfort and nice things to distract you from the Word of God, but I'm not so sure. I knew another woman on the estate who was fifty-five years old, had lost a lung and had an alcohol problem. Her sons kept dogs in the house, and because of the dogs and the terrible smell, workmen who were changing over the heating system refused to install the new equipment. That woman died last winter of hypothermia and not one of us rapped on her door. We didn't love her enough. If we had we'd have been out there on the estate telling people what was going on. Now I think it's harder for that woman to have got her mind off the cold for long enough to read the Gospel than it would be for someone in suburbia.

"We've a young girl who comes in here regularly. She married at sixteen, had a child before she was seventeen, and had a husband in jail. He came out, mugged an old man and she decided to leave him and went to live with another man with three children of his own. Now she can't believe that God wants her with all her problems. Then there's the hunger. I was in a house last week and the woman there had one pound in her purse. A lot of people round here are victims of the loan sharks, the present-day money lenders, and once the 'tick men', as they're known here, come round on a Friday night there's not much money left over for food. The pound note she had was to feed her family over the weekend. Now nobody can convince me that it's harder for people in suburbia, because there it's a straight choice between being selfish and not being selfish, but people here first have to get their whole attention off the hunger and the squalid surroundings for long enough to be able to believe there's a bit of light at the end of the tunnel. They're third generation non-churchgoers so they've no idea what religion means.

"I think it's sometimes a cop out to pray for things when you can actually do something. Sometimes there are things completely outside your control, when all you can do is get down on your knees and ask the Lord for help, but God has no hands, no feet, no mouth and He expects us to be His witnesses. He's putting work right under our noses but quite often we go home to our warm houses and forget it. And the Lord knows there are problems enough here to give us plenty of work for some time yet. I'm sorry to sound so negative but you have to face the issue. You read the book of Nehemiah and you see a great man of prayer and vision, but the first thing he did was to sit down and weep over the ruins. That's what we've got to do. It's no use saying 'Be positive and everything will come right'. We've got to see the ruins and the wreckage we've left around the place over the past fifty years, and work hard to build something out of it. We've got to forget about little groups meeting for an emotional experience, and we've got to be prepared to stand alongside skinheads and drop-outs. I was in charge of the Simon Community [a hostel for homeless men] for two years, and in all that time not one Christian visitor rapped on the door, and I was amazed.

"I can't take the credit for anything I've done, I'm merely God's agent. I started this day-centre and was responsible for the business side of things, like the community work scheme, but I've decided to hand all the administration over to someone else so that I can get involved from morning till night with these people here. I shudder to think what lies in store, but I have to say they're great lads here. Mind you, they'll tell you exactly what they think of you, and they'll bombard you with questions, but they're very generous and with their last fifty pence before dole day they'll offer to buy you a cup of tea. There is goodness here to build on, even despite the strong influence of the organizations. I would say, though, that the biggest social evil here is alcohol. On the day we opened there was a child of eight sitting on the doorstep drunk on four cans of lager. He's eleven now and he's a regular weekend drinker. Alcohol round here is too freely available – it's everywhere, and some people will do anything for drink. In fact when my brother-in-law was shot by the U.D.A. by mistake he was shot by people who at the time were too drunk to recognize a man they'd gone to school with. They walked up behind him and put five bullets in his back.

"I have very little formal relationship with Catholics as such, because I think our reconciliation is in Christ who transcends all the barriers of denomination. I suppose I'm hopeful enough to see just a tiny revival here, a small group of people who are willing to go in where it hurts – into the real inner city areas of East Belfast, the Falls and the Shankill. It came to me in the form of a Bible study two years ago, a feeling that we, like the people of Israel, have to come back to rebuild the Temple – to offer people an alternative and that alternative is the love of Christ.

"The secret of Christianity is what the apostle Paul said, 'I have learnt in all things to be content'. Now sometimes he was beaten, and at other times he was at the top of the twig, but wherever he was he had this contentment. That's what we try to get across to the people who come in here – not an insurance policy or something after death but a living faith for the here and now – a peace and contentment coming from the knowledge that you've put your life in God's hands for Him to guide it. I'm a very poor example of that but I'm trying, and I hope that through Him I'm becoming more loving to my fellow man."

Father Pat Buckley

"Belfast is very much a matriarchal society. The women rule the roost and in comparison the men are quite weak. Maybe it comes from decades of not having jobs and not feeling useful, but it also comes from the violence in this place. If you're a man the paramilitaries can take you out and shoot you or kneecap you, but they won't do that if you're a granny, or an aunt, or a mammy."

Father Pat Buckley, for whom the title "turbulent priest" could have been coined, speaks with respect and affection for these Belfast women whom he made his allies. "They also have tremendous courage. I saw an example of that one night when one of our schools was taken over by the British Army for an election the next day. A hundred fellahs from around here decided they were going to burn the school down with the soldiers in it. I raised a group of about twenty women and they stood in line between the gang and the school, and succeeded in chasing that gang away. When the British Army officer saw what was happening he thought to himself, 'Aha, there are twenty women on our side and friendly', and he brought out some tea for them. They weren't having any of that, though, and they told him to stuff his tea because they didn't give a damn about him and his British soldiers – it was their school they were interested in. Think of it – the Army officer thought he'd made some new Catholic friends!"

It was the women predominantly who constituted Pat Buckley's strength during the time he served as a parish priest on the notorious Divis Estate at the lower end of the Falls Road. Appointed as a "holiday relief" to fill in for three weeks, he stayed for five years, during which time he

71

made many devoted friends and more than a few passionate enemies. He dates his first involvement in the community politics of the Divis from the time of the Hunger Strikes.

"The rioting, the shooting and the bombing gave everybody a tough time on the Falls, and the Hunger Strikes were really the climax to a lot of years of tension. During that period on any day there were dozens of cars hijacked then brought into the Divis and burnt. I remember one day when they got their hands on this huge articulated lorry full of grain, which they up-ended and emptied all over the streets. Now, there were an awful lot of rats around there and what with all this grain around they were running about as big as greyhounds after that. So some of us decided we'd have to do something about it. I got together about fifteen women and we formed a residents' group, with the ultimate aim of pressing for the total demolition of the Divis flats as soon as possible. In the meantime, though, we decided to clean the place up and put a stop to the rioting and the troublemaking on the estate.

"The troublemaking took a number of forms but the most characteristic of Belfast was (and is) the phenomenon of 'joyriding'. This involves the taking and driving away of cars by youngsters aged from twelve upwards. The cars, sometimes driven by boys whose legs were barely long enough to reach the pedals, would end up on the estate before being ransacked for valuable accessories and then set alight. The troublemakers themselves, then as now, are known, in a peculiarly outdated Belfast phrase, as 'the hoods', and are tough, young delinquents with varying degrees of affiliation to the paramilitary organizations.

"We were very successful in reducing the joyriding and other criminal problems to almost nothing. Basically the fifteen women and I went out onto the streets at night, and if anybody was doing any harm we sent them back home. We also went out on the nights that they were going to riot, and we took their petrol bombs off them. There was nothing they could do to a priest and fifteen women – a gang of fifteen fellahs would have been shot or beaten up. That way we gradually stopped the riots and had control of the area."

Such an unorthodox approach to street policing deserves perhaps a moment's explanation, and it is best found in a brief biography of Pat Buckley himself, an unorthodox operator if ever there was one.

Born in Dublin thirty-five years ago he began his training for the priesthood there in 1970. "At that time Vatican II hadn't really begun to be applied and the seminary system hadn't changed. It was just like a prison and we were going into this rigid, repressive system as young people who'd grown up in the sixties with a fair amount of freedom. As a result some of us tended to buck the system, and I suppose I was the chief bucker and they expelled me. After that I was told that no other Irish Bishop would take me on because I was shop-spoiled so to speak. They told me I'd never make a priest – obviously because I would not fit into their mould. Somehow, though, I got into a second seminary in Ireland, finished my training, was ordained in 1976 and, not being welcome in Ireland, went to Wales to work as a priest."

He had always wanted to work in Ireland and so found himself a very unwilling exile in Wales. Not only that, he says, he found himself very lonely in presbyteries there where, as he puts it, "The kind of order of importance in the Catholic Presbytery is this – the parish priest first, then the housekeeper, then the dog, then the curate. You're just a very unwelcome lodger in the parish priest's house. I lived in some very cruel situations and I was very un-happy."

After two years he left Wales, to the considerable dis-pleasure of the Roman Catholic authorities who had in-vested time and money in him only, so they claimed, to be let down by him. This was not to be the last time that Father Buckley and the Establishment did not see eye to eye.

"When I came back I was in a wilderness for nine months or so, not knowing where to go and aware that nobody would have me. So I spent the time working in hostels for down-and-outs and prostitutes in Dublin, saying Mass for them in the morning, and helping out with the chores during the day. I wasn't earning anything then so that was when I decided to go on the dole!"

A priest on the dole! It was yet another measure of Pat Buckley's unorthodox nature.

"They'd never had a priest apply for the dole before in Dublin so they didn't know what to pay me. In the end they decided that as a single person I was worth eleven pounds a week, but when they discovered I was living with my parents they cut it down to four pounds. I queued up regularly for a couple of months, but the queues got so long that I got tired of it and didn't bother.

"At about that time I happened to be visiting a friend in Belfast for the weekend. As I was leaving he expressed his concern for the position I was in and suggested we go to the Bishop to see if anything could be done. I saw the Bishop's assistant and within three days I was appointed to Divis flats as a holiday supply for three weeks, and I heard nothing more from them for five years."

Pat Buckley had – in his own unique style – arrived in Belfast, and on his arrival set about rebuilding morale in the parish to which he had unofficially and unceremoniously been assigned.

"You've got to remember that Divis is one of the worst examples of housing in Europe, so you've got a built-in problem in that you've three or four thousand people living in appalling conditions. Under those circumstances you're bound to have trouble. There are marriage breakdowns, drink problems, drug problems, joyriding, violence, the lot

– and on top of that you've got unemployment at over seventy-five per cent. So you've got people with no money and too much time on their hands hanging around all day long. You couldn't police Divis at the time – you still can't. If two policemen go to Divis to deliver a summons they have to be guarded by twenty armed soldiers, otherwise they'd be beaten up or shot. So if you add all the housing problems to the unemployment and the total lack of law and order, you can imagine the situation. Lifts were being broken, water pipes were being broken, the heating was being switched off so people were suffering greatly. It was total chaos, so it was really necessary for someone to take it in hand.

"When we started our residents' group we were very anxious to exclude the paramilitaries, because the organizations in West Belfast have a tendency to take over everything. We were determined not to let them. And when they came to our meetings we put them out, even though sometimes they came carrying guns. There was one occasion about five or six years ago which was a turning point. One of the paramilitary groups had blown up a soldier on the balcony of one of the blocks of flats, but they also blew up two of our chilldren. After that four hundred mothers and I walked up the road to the I.N.L.A. headquarters and put them out of Divis for good that time. The reason we could do it when others couldn't hinges on the very nature of the paramilitary organizations themselves. Of course there are isolated instances when they come and take over your house for an ambush or an assassination, and it's very dangerous to resist, but the paramilitaries are essentially a guerrilla force which needs cover and the support of the community. If the community rejects them – especially the women – they're finished. That's why I think the way to beat them is not with the British Army but with jobs and decent living conditions and justice. Then they'd be flushed out in no time.

"I was also very involved with the joyriding. We had up to sixty cars a week being driven in here. I would go out and take the cars off the kids and drive them back to the police. I think in a year I must have taken back hundreds of them, and eventually we reduced the problem to, say, one car a month. When they saw me coming they just got out of the cars and ran. I think they were just afraid of me but there was maybe a bit more to it than that. First, I was a priest, and still in places like West Belfast God's holy anointed has a sort of taboo thing about it, and I used that to act from a position of strength. The other thing was that I had a good relationship with the kids, in the sense that when they got into trouble I used to go to court to speak for them. If they were let off they'd be released into my care, or if they were put in prison I'd go and visit them. When I went to Dublin every fortnight to see my family I brought four or five of them with me, and they slept in sleeping bags on the floor of my parents' house. So when they ran from the cars I think they ran because they were ashamed at doing something which they knew I'd disapprove of. The joyriding, though, was almost like an illness with them. I remember having a long chat with one guy before he was taken to court. He eventually agreed to put an end to this joyriding once and for all, and in court he admitted fifty charges. I spoke up for him and at one o'clock he was released into my care, free. At five o'clock the same day he was in another stolen car and had tried to run over a detective sergeant. We did manage to reduce the problem, though, even though it was hard going.

"The only answer to Divis' problems is total demolition. Since we started our work two blocks have been pulled down and another is on its way shortly. So what we did contributed to that demolition, but it was very important to us, at the same time, in such a situation of total hopelessness, to clean the place up and give people self-respect. There are times when you achieve something lasting which is invisible. It may not be as obvious as a block of flats coming down with explosives but it's there when you help people help themselves. If you rekindle people's spirits that's of lasting value.

"The way I look at it is that in this life there are some sufferings which can't be changed – cancer and disease, for example – and in the face of those you need courage and acceptance. When you come across a situation that can be improved, however, then the challenge – whether for a good human being or a Christian – is to make it better. It struck me one day that if we wanted to clean the Divis up all we had to do was go out there and make a start – there and then – to sweep away the excreta, get rid of the broken bedsteads and the mattresses, remove the litter and tin cans, and paint over the graffiti. So one Monday morning I put on my overalls, armed myself with a brush, and started to sweep the streets. Now, the people were very shocked that I was doing this. They weren't having any priest of theirs sweep the streets; so they came out and offered to take the brush off me but I said no. I told them I wanted to keep my brush and that if they wanted to do anything to help they ought to get a brush of their own. By the end of the week we had five hundred brushing, and sweeping, and cleaning.

"It was a bit of a risk now I look back on it, because I had told the committee of the residents' association that it would be a good idea for a big clean-up but there didn't seem to be that much enthusiasm. On the Sunday night before it happened I was lying in bed thinking it was all going to be a total flop. It does sound crazy that going out with a brush in your hand can begin something big, but very often it's a simple notion which can have great significance. And it did. We had several clean-ups and festivals, and spirits were raised. People began to take pride in things. The housing executive gave us three thousand pounds' worth of paint, and the city council sent up a hundred and fifty brushes and shovels. On that first day we filled fifteen skips of rubbish. In fact the Falls Road depot ran out of paint, so I had to drive over to the Shankill in the van myself – wearing my clerical collar and overalls. They were quite surprised to see a Catholic priest at first, but I became a regular visitor and we became friends.

"There are an increasing number of people wanting to reach out. For instance tonight in Larne – which is a *very* Protestant town – we're having an Easter vigil and there are Catholics and Protestants coming along. There are lots of little visible signs of things happening, or people meeting. That can only help matters, but at the same time the politicians here are paralysed by their extremism – they've a kind of tunnel vision. There's a need for a new kind of leadership and it has to be a moral leadership. And that's where I see the churches playing a great role, which so far, I believe, they've failed to do completely. The Church has never wanted to get its hands dirty. I remember an occasion in one inner city presbytery where I was when a priest drew me aside and took me to the window. He parted the curtains, gestured towards the run-down houses in the distance and said, 'You see the people out there. They're as thick as bottled pig shit. All they're short of doing is eating themselves. For years we've tried to do something and failed; they're beyond hope. So don't hurt your head trying to do any more. Pull the curtains, get in front of the TV, get a glass in your hand and enjoy life till you're moved out of here.' I was very shocked at that kind of cynicism, being young and full of idealism. I think the Church has failed these people. I mean, you've got the Catholic Church which basically wants to create and keep an Irish Catholic Ireland where the Bishops will dictate the morality, the constitution and the ethics of the society. On the other hand, you've the Protestant denominations, with their Ministers of the Orange Order marching on the 12th, which want a Protestant Loyalist Ulster for a Protestant

Loyalist people. And between those extremes there's only a façade of improvement.

"I think we have to stop having our own exclusive schools. I really believe that if you put two kids together at the age of four and have them sit together for the next fourteen years they're not going to hate each other. In the Divis flats there are young people who've never met a Protestant in their lives, who don't know what a Protestant Minister is. There was one day when I was showing a group of fifteen Protestant clergy around the flats. One of them, a Methodist, had his collar on and this wee, young girl was standing on the balcony and said to him, 'Are you a priest?'

"And he said, 'No, love, I'm a Protestant. Do you like Protestants?'

"'No, we hate them.'

"'Why do you hate them?'

"'Cos you don't believe in Jesus.'

"And he says, 'Well, I believe in Jesus.'

"So she turns round and says, 'You're a queer Protestant then.'

She was only about seven. Out of the mouths of babes and sucklings! You see, there's a fierce amount of ignorance here which feeds the hatred. I think integrated schools are vital. Some of my own leaders will talk about embracing Protestants, and the way they talk about it could make you weep, but when it comes to integrated education they'll simply refuse to give up their own Catholic schools.

"It's the same in reverse with some Protestants. I'm very suspicious of this born-again thing, because for me Christianity is about struggling for a lifetime in response to an invitation. It involves a lot of sweat, a lot of falling and getting up again. I know it happened to St Paul, but it's very unreal to me that at nine o'clock at night in your room your bed shakes and you're thrown down on your knees and from then on it's all beauty and love and glory. I think it's a very narrow thing to say that if you're not a Baptist or an Elim Pentecostal or whatever then you're heading for the roaring fires of Hell. I think that's anti-Christian and there's an awful lot of that around in Belfast.

"I also think my own church has been hijacked by the modern day Pharisees. I believe in the kernels of the Catholic faith – the Eucharist, and the Sacraments, Scripture and the Priesthood and so on – but I still think the church has been taken out of the hands of the people and hijacked by a select few, who for a price will give people what Christ gave them for nothing. So I have two options. Either I leave the system or I stay in and change it. Well, I have stayed in and agitated and generally been a thorn in the Establishment's side, and I have been criticized for having a poor relationship with my colleagues and an over-involvement in social issues. But it's very hard not to be heavily involved in social issues in Northern Ireland.

"For instance, there was one evening when I was running a disco for the local kids, when halfway through there was a knock on the door and two masked men – one with a revolver and one with a sawn-off shotgun – were standing there. They called me outside and put the revolver to my head. Well, I thought that was going to be it because I figured they were Protestant paramilitaries coming in retaliation for a couple of policemen who'd just recently been killed. So I was pretty sure I was for the high jump that night, but it turned out they were Republican para-militaries wanting the takings from the disco, and I refused to hand them over. They pushed me back into the hall and I managed to rush to the back, lock the money in the safe, and climb out through the back window. All this time the disco is blaring away. I ran across some fields and called the police, and when I came back along the road the men had taken over the stage and put all the lights on. The kids were lined up round the hall and these fellahs were shouting for me, saying they'd shoot me dead and that if they didn't get me that time then everyone was to come to 10 o'clock Mass the following Sunday and they'd see a priest being shot during Mass. When I came back one of the guys asked me if I'd been for the police and I said, 'Yes, why don't you stay around for a short while? Because you've been very courageous so far amongst people who are unarmed and I'd like to see what you're like when the police come.' At that point they pushed past and called me a Loyalist bastard. So I just said, 'If you guys are what's going to run Ireland when we're free, God help us!' They hopped into a car and as they drove off the police arrived and they passed each other, but I got the car number and the following day they were arrested. They turned out to be two young parishioners of mine. I still see them, but the first time I visited them they were embarrassed. They told me the guns were loaded and when I asked if they intended to shoot they said, 'We'd decided that if you'd pulled the masks off us we'd have shot you dead.'

"My record for fighting injustices by the state is also quite good and that's the reason why I'm not a Republican target. I'm known as someone who has fought the 'supergrass' system, for example. Last September we sat for a week outside the Crumlin Road Jail in protest at the injustices of it, and that's not the first time I've been critical of the police and the authorities.

"I would stand a hundred per cent against violence from the I.R.A. in pursuit of a united Ireland. But having said that I'd add that you have got to meet people – like Gerry Adams, for example – whose views you don't necessarily share. While I'm opposed to the violence of the I.R.A. I can understand it. It's a symptom of a problem which goes very deep, and which rests on decades of injustice which has festered in Belfast and elsewhere. Whenever you have that you'll also have the outpouring of the evil of paramilitary violence. I think it's hypocritical of church people to condemn the men of violence (which is a symptom), and not to condemn the injustice which provokes them (which is the disease). And remember that for centuries the Church made the awful mistake of teaching that it's OK to kill in a just war, which they described as, in some ways, a defensive war. Well, the I.R.A. would say that they are fighting a just war, they would say that the British have attacked them and that according to the theology of the Church they're entitled to wage a defensive war against the British.

"From the point of view of being a Christian in faith I have tremendous hope for Belfast and the North of Ireland. I really think it's a huge international Christian scandal that fellow Christians are fighting each other and for no particular reason. I think within the next twenty years it's going to be transformed. Certainly within my lifetime I would say that reason will triumph over irrationality, and that more and more convinced Christians will surface and overcome all this false religious stuff. And then what is now an international scandal will become an example of healing. For that you need prayer and action. I would be concerned about any prayer which did not find its way into action. It's the same with love. If you get an oxygen tent, put yourself inside it and fill it up with love and prayer, what good does that do? There's a contradiction somewhere. You have to remove the tent and let love reproduce itself. You can't lock it up tight, you have to let love give itself away all the time. And the more love you let out, the more love it will generate. In just the same way do you send your prayers up to God and your actions out to people.

"Part of my work has been forming the residents' group and dealing with the joyriding problem in the Divis. I'd always said that if a priest didn't look after the kids then the Provos would. They want anarchy because it suits their purpose, and I think the Church is the only one strong enough to deprive them of that role. Most priests don't want to bother.

"On the Divis you have to bother. Take the time we had the festival, and people from the paramilitaries turned up armed. Now I had to go up to the headquarters and ask them to pull out. It was very easy to get killed that night, but in my position I had to go up there and know just who to talk to. For instance, I remember a young parishioner coming up to me – he was only about eighteen and he had raped a girl, another eighteen-year-old. He was terrified because he had been sentenced by them to be shot through the head. Now, obviously I would totally disapprove of rape but to be shot for it is an extreme punishment, and so I had to know where to go and who to contact to get that execution stopped. In the end his punishment was commuted to going round a dozen drinking clubs on a Saturday night with a couple of armed men and standing on a stage and publicly describing what he had done. The whole thing was designed to be a total disgrace for him in front of the whole community. My purpose was to be someone whom people knew and could rely on in times of emergency and crisis.

"There was another occasion when someone connected with the organization came along to confession, and told me that according to the word going round a particular person was going to be killed. Now the person in the confessional had a conscience problem with it so we talked, and finally between the two of us it was agreed that I should warn the police. So I told the police about it and between us we saved the person from being set up, ambushed and executed.

"If you want to show the hope here, you've got to be aware of the cruelty. If you have to go into a flat and pick up the bits of brain belonging to a twelve-year-old or see a soldier lying dead, or someone who's been shot, you know what I mean when I say 'cruelty'. There are wounds here, there is cruelty here – it's everywhere for the eye to see in the North. So there's hope and there's cruelty here at the same time and, strangely enough, that's one of the reasons I love working here. If I was working as a priest in Dublin or London I'd basically be very comfortable and quiet, and probably the biggest enemy I'd have would be apathy. Whereas here, because of the troubles, all those top layers of flesh have been stripped back, as it were, and you're left looking at the vital organs of life."

Three Communities

Cornerstone

The first meeting with Isabel Hunter came as a surprise. The day-centre was full of noise. The television played loudly in one corner, the tea bar was working at full stretch, serving egg and chips or beans on toast to a room packed full of people chatting and passing the time of day. At the far end a group of large, tough, amiable young men was absorbed in a game of snooker, their enthusiasm reaching a crescendo with every half-decent shot or near miss. An irreverent, impromptu commentary on this and a game of pool nearby filled the room, while older men, apparently oblivious to the din, sat at tables drinking tea and exchanging news.

Into this predominantly male lunchtime congregation stepped Isabel, accompanied by two other middle-aged women, nuns in "civvies" as it turned out – the first of a number of surprises! The "Loyalist" boys at the far end played on, giving their entrance not even a first glance, let alone a second. Why should they? On the face of it there was nothing remarkable to see. But there was something remarkable about the events leading up to Isabel's decision to work here at this day-centre on the Shankill Road; and something undeniably hopeful, too, about the motivation of this softly-spoken, demure, former school teacher who gave up a job and a home to help the unemployed and under-privileged of this corner of Belfast.

"I suppose you could say my work here is in prayer, really", she says. It is a surprising remark in view of the fact that she is ready to turn her energies to anything and not unafraid to get her hands dirty in the ordinary, every-day tasks the day-centre demands. The remark is doubly surprising, however, in the context in which it is delivered. A noisy hall full of unemployed young men, in the heart of one of the city's most notorious flashpoints, is hardly the place, one thinks, to find an ex-school mistress expounding on the value of the contemplative life in her day to day work. So how did Isabel Hunter come to be here in the first place?

"It all began about twelve years ago when I was at a church in Knock and it so happened that Bill Jackson (the minister in charge of the Mission) was speaking. He told us all of his work on the Shankill Road, and the thing that struck me was the deprivation of many of the elderly folk and the bad conditions they were living under. I remember him speaking of one old lady, for instance, who had rats running across her bed. Now at that time I had just finished nursing a very sick aunt who had been very close to me. She had brought me up and really been like a mother to me, and it struck me very much that I would have hated her to be living under those conditions. I was teaching at a primary school at the time, and although I took a lot of things away with me from the service that night the dominant image I came away with was of this old lady and the rats.

"Shortly after that I was driving my little niece home, and all the time I was thinking of that sermon. All the time I was thinking how strange it was that somebody wouldn't give an old person like that a house. I suppose I was thinking of somebody who perhaps had several houses and who wouldn't miss one of them, when suddenly into my mind came the thought, 'There's your house!' At that time I was considering selling or letting my own home, because I was about to set off for Germany where I intended to teach for a couple of years.

"I prayed about it for a long time and finally offered it to Bill, if he thought it would be of any use. It was a small semi-detached in Knock, which was some miles away from

Belfast, and we decided that money would be better than a house so far away in Knock. So I decided to sell it, and after the mortgage had been paid off the rest of the money went to the Mission. Bill subsequently used it as a fund for opening up a couple of houses which had been bricked up nearby. Then he renovated them and used them for housing old people."

All of this meant, of course, that Isabel's financial security had gone in a sacrifice which many might have thought rather foolhardy – especially as she was embarking on an "adventure" abroad with only the prospect of a short-term teaching contract to guarantee an income. But that was not how she herself viewed it.

"I suppose you could say I needed the money to settle in Germany, but I was so clear in my mind that it really didn't come into the calculations. The thought of giving up the house came to me in a blinding flash, and after my eyes had got accustomed to the light, as it were, I did begin to wonder if it was the right thing to do. But after talking to Bill and after much prayer I knew that it was. I've never doubted it since. You'll never know a hundred per cent for a fact that a thought or an action is from God, but there are moments when you can be as sure as it's possible to be in this life that God is behind your decisions, and I'd say, looking back, that what has happened since that time has confirmed God's hand in it all.

"At the end of my two years in Germany I wasn't sure whether to come back or stay on. Then into my mind one day came the words, 'What do ye more than others? I have much for you to do', and again, I felt, they came in a way which you cannot doubt is from outside you. There were question-marks over my staying on in Germany at the time. My father was still alive and it wasn't fair leaving my brother and his wife with all the responsibility for looking after him. That increased the doubts I had. None the less I went on applying for jobs abroad and, deep down, was pleased not to get them. So all this confirmed me in my decision to return.

"When I came back to Northern Ireland I had the feeling that there was something for me to do here over and above the teaching I'd been trained for. Then one evening, again at a service in Knock, Cecil Kerr from the Renewal Centre was preaching, and he said that there was someone in the congregation to whom God wanted to make a blessing. It was then that it struck me that the blessing was for me and had some connection with the Mission – although since the business with the house I'd had nothing really to do with it. So I wrote to Bill to see if there was anything I could do to help. By this time I'd got another job in a local school, and I suggested that perhaps I could use my car to run elderly people to the Mission evenings on Thursday. I felt that God could be using this voluntary work as a way of saying to me that I should consider leaving teaching to do this full-time. Shortly after, a letter came round the staff room saying that anybody over fifty could apply for redundancy. So I did and here I am."

At present Isabel shares a house with Evelyn Whyte, a deaconess, who started working on the Shankill after a period teaching Indian immigrants in Birmingham.

"My first reaction when I was assigned to the Mission," says Evelyn, "was, 'Oh dear! What have I let myself in for here?' but I soon realized this was the right place for me to be. Isabel and I took out a joint mortgage on this house, which we both use as a base for our work. The house has a great peace about it. Our purpose is to reach out to the community in practical ways like providing employment and drop-in centres, and also to visit homes and care for people in general ways, showing them there is a better life and there is hope."

Now before people begin to wonder how it is that Isabel could afford a joint mortgage on a house when she had sold up and given away her own before, financially speaking, casting herself adrift on open seas, let Isabel herself explain – in characteristic understatement.

"Well, it's very strange," she says with mild bewilderment, "but a friend whom I had met in Germany and to whom I'd become very close was suddenly bereaved, and her husband had died leaving what turned out to be a very valuable stamp collection. Now although it wasn't in any way as if I wanted it – and I'd never suggested I needed it – when my friend sold the collection, quite out of the blue she offered me the money that it had raised. It was really astonishing. I think she had it in mind that I might use it to buy a house."

It should be obvious by now whose guiding hand Isabel saw in all this. What others see as mere coincidence she views as evidence of a greater, more substantial plan.

"I wouldn't distinguish between the social and the spiritual work we do here. One sign of hope I see is in 'Cornerstone' which we set up three years ago and where Catholics and Protestants meet. We all felt that God was calling on us to form a religious community, and so with a nucleus of people living in and around the Shankill, Cornerstone was officially launched.

"We really think of ourselves as a praying community of people from all different backgrounds. Our ages range from twenty-four to eighty and we meet once a week at the moment because everyone is so busy with their daily, more practical ministry of social work, counselling or whatever. So while on the one hand we're involved in all sorts of activity we're also concerned to have a quieter, more contemplative side to it all. Prayer changes things. It's at the heart of all our work here and through it we can see God's Spirit in action. We have a great awareness of the praying communities of the past – such as the Benedictines. Their motto 'For God alone my Soul waits in silence' is one we all take to heart – even in the often hectic days on the Shankill. The effect of prayer is incalculable; we've no idea what terrible things it has prevented or what good things it has caused. It's a mystery. It's not just asking for things; it's giving yourself up to God's Will, putting aside your own wishes and your own thoughts. And then it's somehow praying that Will into action. I'm not saying I've reached that point yet – not by a long way – all we can say is that we're in the early stages of it. I know you can say that compared to the thousands who live on the Shankill a handful of people of good-will and faith meeting for prayer is a drop in the ocean, but we will never know the effect we have.

"Let me give you one small instance. When they had the last Loyalist strike in protest at the Anglo-Irish Agreement there was tension on the streets. It was an eerie sensation on that day, as we were holding a prayer meeting at the Mission – nothing at all to do with Cornerstone, as it happened. We kept the doors locked but had the lights on and I wondered how they would react when they knew we were open. When we came out there were cars burning. Beer kegs were being thrown at police and there were groups of people standing around. I was very frightened by it all. After it had all died down we were speaking to one lad who normally finds it very difficult NOT getting involved in trouble – as soon as there's a riot, he's there joining in – and he told us that he didn't feel inclined to get involved that night. Now, we had been praying specially for him because we knew what he was like. So you could ask 'Did our prayer have any effect? Did our prayer stop him joining in the riot?' I think it may have.

"What I found scary that night was that they were just standing around watching – like it was a show or a play. It was worrying to see that that was their approach to life – watching cars burn and police being attacked. I felt that there was something very wrong here. A riot is an unpredictable thing and it can be transformed in a moment. I think a clerical collar can sometimes help to defuse things and I think prayer can do the same.

"It's not always easy getting through to people on the

Shankill, and when it comes to joint meetings of both denominations my impression is that Catholics are more open than we Protestants here. Shankill Road 'Prods' are very much against mixing. They've grown up with the feeling that the Catholics are doctrinally wrong, and the churches have all played their part in that process. When I was sixteen I remember hearing a series of sermons on the errors of Rome. That was a very common occurrence then and it left its mark. The only grounds for hope are in Christ, but it seems to me we're going to have to go through a great deal of suffering before we realize this."

The Shankill Road Mission

If Cornerstone represents the still centre of reconciliation on the Shankill, then the Shankill Road Mission represents the powerful cutting edge of social witness and Christian evangelism. The man in charge is a Presbyterian Minister, Bill Jackson, who has been there since the present "troubles" began. At sixty he still looks youthful and fit but although he has the spare, muscular frame of a retired sprinter he gives the constant impression of weariness; weariness not in the sense of being worn out or washed out and good for nothing more, but weariness as of a man tired at the end of a long, hard day spent in the service of others. Achievement here is hard won, progress is slow and acknowledgement sporadic. It *is* a tiring life.

"It's inevitable that the clergy keeps itself pretty much to itself in a busy parish like this one. You've got so much to attend to that at times you feel like a juggler trying to keep a dozen balls in the air at one time. As far as our everyday work goes the ecumenical ball doesn't do much flying about because we've got enough to do looking after the local people here. Although things have changed a lot since the late nineteenth century, when this Mission was founded, there's a sense of sameness in the Shankill – a sense of feeling embattled, of people feeling shut in on themselves and not really understanding what's going on. People talk about the working classes having fallen away from Church but I doubt if they ever really were in the Church. They're certainly outside the Presbyterian Church, and I'd say this Mission is exceptional in that it's making headway in what is a working-class area.

"One of the problems we have is that most of those who

worship on a Sunday, or those who come to a Friday night service and prayer meeting, would probably be from working-class origins but they've done well and moved up the road a bit. There's a tremendous difference between Woodvale on the Upper Shankill and the Lower Shankill where we are. But that sort of thing happens everywhere and I mean no criticism by it. Christianity does make people more thoughtful, more positive, more thrifty, and they tend to move away from their old attitudes of living for today and letting tomorrow bring what it will. I suppose you'd say it is the people from up the road who make up the backbone of our congregation, whereas the people we deal with day to day are those in the drop-in centre – the unchurched, those suspicious of the very word 'Christian'. They're afraid of people pushing religion down their throats. For them it's just rules and regulations and they're not going to have any of that. But they've also got a pretty poor opinion of Christians. Christians are middle-class, a race apart. They're easily put off by religion so we've had to be cautious about it to them. Perhaps we've been over-cautious about it, but better that than rushing our fences and scaring them off. Our big problem at first was how we could get to speaking to them, how we could present the Gospel to them. Sure, you can hand out tracts and go knocking on doors – which we've done – but your success is limited. Back in the '70s we had an evangelist working full-time with us. He was very good but he got practically nowhere, except with drunks and suicide cases and people in the lowest strata, the outcasts, if you like. Yet many in the Shankill are decent, ordinary people who are completely outside the Church. It's a long uphill struggle.

"In the early '70s I decided to pack in the ministry altogether. I was working in Townsend Street just down from here, and I felt the congregations were just going nowhere. My friends on the road who were not Christians used to say to me, 'What are you going in there for? Those people in there have no concern for us at all.' It wasn't really fair to blame them, though. OK, they came in on Sunday from all around and they went away again, but you've got to remember that those were the worst days of the 'troubles' and they couldn't get in for evening activities. Even if they had, though, it would have been just their own kind of evening activity with no relevance to anybody else outside. So I seriously considered leaving all this behind and paying my way as a social worker.

"Then a friend of mine, who's a good deal wiser than I am, started to tell me about the influence a minister has even yet. Of course it's not the same as it was when I started in the '50s, when you'd get a wee fellah doffing his cap to you! And even then that was dying out. But I think he was right. The Church, with all its weaknesses, is an inevitable part of the Gospel. People who commit themselves to Christ have to be seen to be standing together. I suppose we reached our lowest ebb in 1979 when we had a congregation set in its ways and always looking back to the old days, a congregation demoralized by the troubles and redevelopment. I always felt, even in the most despairing moments, it had to be there. I suppose talking to my friend convinced me I had to be there as well.

"We have seen some progress recently. Our social witness goes hand in hand with the Gospel, and so as well as looking after the soul we try to look after the body too. We formed a housing association in the '70s and developed a lot of housing for the elderly. We've a little co-operative making bits of furniture, and we've got little work teams which go out and help redecorate people's houses. We used to have a big dinner every year for about three hundred and fifty, and we had this tradition going way back to the '20s when everybody got a parcel. But the whole scheme had got out of hand and had turned into a shambles because there was so much greed. You'd get these wee scraps of paper handed in from people saying they needed a parcel, and then when you went along to them you'd find the house coming down with possessions. It was getting to be such a racket that I was glad when we stopped it. We run a number of A.C.E. schemes here (Action for Community Employment) which have been very successful and given people who were unemployed a couple of years' paid work. We've forty of them running at the moment, and they've had their spin-offs. Some of the young lads have been coming pretty regularly for three years now.

"On the Shankill we're known as the Albert Hall, and although people know it as a Christian body I'm not sure how many people link it specifically with the Church. They're very vague on things like that. You find people do tend to come in for one thing and then ask for another when they realize the church connections. I've had a number of lads coming in and asking me to baptize their children, but when I go round I'll find it's just a common-law marriage. Then I have the awful job of saying that in all conscience I just can't do it. But I suppose, to look on the positive side, these problems wouldn't arise were it not for the fact that they at least see me around and get to know me a bit. There was this wee girl with a baby she wanted baptized. I had baptized her sister-in-law's three children, but this young girl wasn't married so I told her I couldn't go ahead. Well, she got on her high horse a bit and the repercussions of this were that, well, she was going to stop paying into the church and would stop sending in the envelopes! But I notice now she wants me to baptize her new baby so perhaps she's forgotten and forgiven me.

"Our various community schemes and our evangelism do represent some progress but we've an awful lot to work against. One of the experiences I've never forgotten was when I was in Townsend Street and taking the funeral of two U.V.F. men blown up by a bomb they were carrying in their car. I'd known one of them; he'd been in the Boys'

Brigade and had been brought up in the Church. In fact, over a period of four years there were twelve people killed with some sort of connection with the Church. But what made the funeral so harrowing was that the widow had not seen the body. Normally it would be laid out in the house and a little service held before the lid was screwed on. In this case though the coffin had been sealed before it came into the house, and the first thing that happened was that she wanted the lid off. And one of the men said to me, 'It's only bits and pieces in there, we can't take it off'.

"As if that wasn't bad enough, what I saw when we came out of the service has stayed with me since. It's only at a football match that I've seen so many young men together. It seemed to me that there was a mile-long procession of men. And they were quiet. They looked on the dead man as a hero – someone who had died for his belief. Now what has happened to those young men? I suppose a lot of them will be in prison now. How do you bring the Gospel to these people? If they've not got blacks to hate they've got Catholics!

"The young people here in their twenties and thirties are tremendously limited. You can almost see them looking over their shoulder. For example, a young lad came into the Mission with a note telling him to go to the Royal Victoria Hospital on the Falls Road. I asked him when he had his appointment and he said, 'Oh, I'm not going. I wouldn't go up there!' In the end we had to take him up ourselves by car.

"You notice it, too, when you take these youngsters out of Belfast rock climbing or canoeing. You find them almost sighing with relief. You can see them changing. They stop this constant looking behind them and start to relax a bit. It's then you see some of the pressures these lads are under – pressures on them which they hardly realize themselves.

"The drinking clubs put a lot of pressure on them – in fact last year when we had a mission to the Shankill one of our big achievements was to go inside one of them – a desperate place! – and hold a rally. We had this American girl singing and we had a couple of converts that night. Now, I'm a man with a lot of difficulties about this sort of evangelism and I'm certainly against this continual psychological pressurizing and emotionalism, but the man we had as our evangelist is someone who has really been called to be an evangelist and he is very convincing. Despite my initial reserve I thought to myself afterwards that because of the state some of these lads are in they really do have to be pressurized; that it takes something out of the ordinary to really hit them. With the Gospel you can easily overstep the mark and pile on the pressure, but in circumstances like this in the Shankill maybe we don't go far enough. And I became convinced that some of the converts we got (and are now nurturing in the Mission here) need something like that almost to *push* them into a new life.

"There was a lad who came to the front at the end of the meeting, and I went round to see him the following day. He told me he'd planned to go off to a football match and he knew that if he did it would be the same routine of going to the pub afterwards, and the night before would be just a dream. So then I arrived and he told me how he had a couple of cases (both involving drink and drugs) hanging over him. He had intended to plead not guilty but after last night he said he was going to plead guilty. So in the end I went with him to court just to be able to say I'd seen a genuine change. My heart sank when I heard the magistrate say, 'You have an appalling record going back for years!' I wondered what I had let myself in for. Anyway, I told the magistrate that I genuinely felt he had had a conversion experience and that we were doing all we could for him, and he got a three-year suspended sentence which I don't think he would have got if I hadn't been there. Well, the lad's got a job now in the day-centre and he's doing well at the moment. We have a few new Christians there – all young men who've been out of work a long time.

"I think of another young lad. An awfully likeable big fellah who comes from a family where there's not a shred of Christianity – every Friday night, the old mother's drunk – and he's started coming in here. That's where the hope is, in these people turning away from their old lives. And in them all I've seen their attitudes to Catholics change. They drink the bitterness in with their mothers' milk and, of course, the fewer Catholics they know the more bitter they are. But the Gospel can deal with that – I've seen it.

"I mean, even last summer we had three or four fellahs who came to the meetings in the new Methodist Church. Now for them even to go through the door of a church a year ago would have been unthinkable. And they came back three times. One fellah couldn't make it because he'd been kneecapped in both legs and was in hospital for a while, but one of the Americans went to visit him. When I went up there he was still talking about it. He couldn't understand why anybody should bother to go up and see him. We believe that if and when there's a breakthrough there'll be a domino effect. I think I have more hope now than ten years ago and that's why I mentioned those fellahs following the coffin – that was the low point for me. I think you've got to earn the right to speak the Gospel to people by helping them with their everyday problems and I think we're doing that now. We're beginning to earn that right."

*

One family which has gone through its share of suffering – and come out wiser on the other side – is the Strain family, Charlie and Agnes, and their four children. Charlie's is very much a success story of the Mission and he is the walking proof that its work can and does alter people's lives.

Like many people living in the small terraced houses where the kerbstones are painted red, white and blue, and the gable ends boast garish pictorial tributes to "King Billy" and Ulster's Protestant ascendancy, Charlie rarely if ever met any Catholics.

"I knew nothing about them. I thought they worshipped wee idols and that their God was different from ours. Not that I believed in God myself at the time – or not in any real way. That was before I became a Christian."

Now, eight years after giving up the drink and cutting his loose links with the Protestant paramilitaries, Charlie is a changed man, and his family all the happier and all the more stable for it. It looks almost certain that he will be unemployed again very shortly when his short-term community job comes to an end, but he will doubtless continue to work as a volunteer at the Mission where he became the first A.C.E. worker three years ago and where he is now a valued member of the Christian social work team.

The family's association with the Mission began ten years ago when Charlie's alcoholism was getting worse. His wife, Agnes, recalls going along there for help for the children when all the money had gone on drink and when she was finding the going tough. Then after a spell drying out and a genuine spiritual conversion, Charlie changed.

"He used to spend almost as much time in church as he did in the pub", says Agnes with a smile. "I told him to take his bed down there!"

Nowadays, though, Agnes herself spends a lot of her time at the Mission's day-centre as a volunteer behind the tea bar, or simply as one of those on hand to do anything that's needed. Naturally shy people, both she and Charlie feel being there has taught them a lot about how to get on with others.

As Charlie explains, "These boys have all done the same as me – drinking, betting on horses, getting involved with the paramilitaries and all the rest of it associated with having too much time on your hands and being up to no good. But for some reason or other they were able to make me aware I was a Christian – being with them gave me that assurance when I was unsure of it myself. I used to think it was a one-day thing, you know, being a Sunday Christian, but then I started to discover that it was seven days a week, twenty-four hours a day. And your home and your family life begin to change when you realize those things.

"Looking back, I think that coming off the drink was swapping one kind of attention for another. In the pub you wanted people around you, and if you had money you could get it by buying a few drinks and all drinking together. At first it was the same in the church. All the congregation would be flocking around me giving me the same attention I'd wanted when I was drinking – only this time I didn't need money to get it. Then there were the times I'd be asked to paint somebody's house, and all the time I thought I was praising the Lord for it. But I wasn't. In actual fact I was taking the praise for myself and enjoying the attention I was getting. Well, pretty soon I realized I was on the wrong road here. Better start doing it for the Lord's glory, not mine.

"And the point is that the boys we get in here can see whether you're doing things for the right reasons, and if they don't like what they see they'll tell you straight. You've got to be honest to them and true to your faith – there are no back doors. You can't teach love, you have to show it by your example. The lads we get in here are hard fellahs; they'll join in a riot at the drop of a hat, and when there's tension you can feel it on the streets and feel it in the day-centre."

It is a tension which affects not only energetic youths in the city but small children as well, and bringing up a family here is an effort and a worry.

"At the first sign of any trouble", says Agnes "we're out looking for the kids to bring them back in. For instance, we had a riot on the street the other night and as soon as I heard the thumps and bangs we went out for Nat and Sam [two of their sons aged fifteen and thirteen]. They weren't throwing stones (or if they were, they stopped when they saw me), they were just standing there watching this car burning. So I brought them back in. Even if they're innocent the police won't always know, and once they start charging up the Road and firing plastic bullets then anyone running with the crowd can be in the firing line. In situations like that innocent children can get in the way – it's happened before. All the things the kids see round here must affect them. There was the time a couple of years ago when a few of them were playing on the soldiers' armoured cars. They shouldn't have been but that's the sort of thing kids will do round here. One of them jumped on, lost his grip and was crushed underneath the wheels. Now our youngest, Joanne, was there at the time and saw it all, and for a long time after that she would wet the bed. A lot of the violence does get to them, it's bound to."

Yet despite it all the Strain household survives intact. A year ago I was privileged to spend some time living with them, sharing their lives, and following them through the day. It begins, incidentally, with a short Bible reading delivered unceremoniously and somewhat diffidently by Charlie as they prepare for school and the day-centre. The elder sons, Charles and Nat, are the serious ones, contemplating an uncertain future in an even more uncertain job market. Joanne, still the baby of the family, smiles constantly and stays close to her mother, while Sam can be relied on to leave a trail of toys, discarded bicycles and roller skates behind him. In short they are an ordinary family and welcoming beyond measure. There is nothing surprising about their warmth, their friendliness and their demonstrative Christian charity; theirs is the unremarkable family life that provides one of the surest and most lasting signs of hope in Belfast. There are tens of thousands of families not unlike the Strains in every ghetto, on both sides of the Peace Line, and the hope of the city's Christian missions is to reach out somehow to them all.

Columbanus

The atmosphere along the Antrim Road running northwards out of Belfast is quite different from that of the Shankill. This is a mixed area of Catholic and Protestant, a more prosperous quarter of the city, where semi-detached and detached houses with generous gardens give the impression of relaxed normality away from the tensions of the "religious" ghettoes. It is here that the Columbanus Community stands. Margaret Wilkinson, a Presbyterian and Evangelical, a former missionary and a woman of formidable intellectual powers, explains its purpose.

"The purpose of this community is to have Catholics and Protestants *living* together as an example of the fact that it can be done. We work out our prayer life together so that we have a place where people who might not easily meet elsewhere can meet. Then from this house we all go out to our various churches (and to each other's) where we will also help in practical ways. I don't think of this as a contemplative order. My whole background and tradition mix the practical and the spiritual. When I was working in a children's home and hospital in India there were about nine hundred of us living together and we were accustomed to community prayer daily – and that is the model we try to adhere to faithfully here in this house."

Margaret Wilkinson's work is for reconciliation in its fullest sense, aware though she is of the doctrinal differences that keep both sides apart. Those doctrinal differences reached a noisy and disturbing climax at the recent visit of Cardinal Suenens of Belgium to St Anne's Cathedral in the city. Outside, protesters maintaining the truth of the Reformed Protestant faith held banners opposing the alleged heresy of the Cardinal's visit; inside, other protesters, positioned strategically throughout the congregation, disrupted the service with shouts of derision and hatred. Although Margaret Wilkinson is dismayed by such antagonism she cannot fail to understand it, coming as she does from the same Reformation tradition and aware as much of its strengths as of its weaknesses.

"For us commitment to Christ was always a crisis, while the Roman Catholics maintained you became a Christian at baptism and so didn't have to know what we called 'real' conversion. And that's why I can understand how those outside the cathedral could do what they did. It saddened me all the more because I know these people and I know their value. You can't serve in Christian missions abroad without knowing the tremendous backing that these very people give in prayer. The faithful mission prayer meetings that go on weekly or monthly; the groups simply coming together to pray for individual missionaries daily and by name – you can't be abroad without valuing those Protestant people of Northern Ireland. You think of their generous giving, their concern for you, their belief in what you're doing – how can you not admire it? And yet when I came back I found myself unable to identify with them wholly because I felt they weren't open to what I feel we need to be open to: to the fact that the Spirit of God can be at work within the Catholic Church.

"I was in India in the '40s and then, of course, there'd been no Vatican II. Ireland was very conservative, and priests and nuns would regard me as a heretic. There was no way their church could reach out to me, so that in church situations Protestants couldn't relate at all to Catholics. You'll find Protestant people all over saying, 'Oh, we had good Catholic neighbours and it's not fair to say there wasn't a friendship; there's always been friendship.' And that would be so in many cases, but on the formal level it was not the case. For instance, I was at the

High School, and when the Convent moved to its new premises closer to us we thought it would be a good idea to have joint games matches. We got the headmistress to approach the Convent to see if it might be possible. Well, I don't know what the reason was – it could have been that they wanted to play Gaelic games rather than the hockey or tennis which we played, or perhaps the Mother Superior didn't want to open things up – but either way the answer was 'no'.

"When I first came to this community I thought I would spend most of my time down at the bottom end of the Antrim Road, in a predominantly Catholic area where I could work across the barriers knowing I was united with Catholic people here. But I've come to find that the more worthwhile thing for me is to go back among the Protestant people – to missionary gatherings, conventions, and rallies – to show them I am still identified with them, that my faith is still basically their faith but that I can live with Catholic people without compromising that faith. That's their great fear. They're afraid that if they appear on religious platforms they'll be giving assent to all that the Catholic church teaches. I believe I can recognize a oneness with Catholics in spite of some of the things in their church which I certainly can't accept. But then, of course, I'm not really in touch with the extreme sections of my own community, nor with those people who, as Catholics, stand behind the I.R.A.

"There are many small things drawing people together here in Belfast. The candle we light at our prayers here in Columbanus is a reminder of that. But God takes small things and uses them. That's where I see the signs of hope.

"Our work also takes us into schools – assemblies, R.E. groups, A-level classes and so on. We were down at the Catholic boys' school recently and they were interested that I, as a lay person, had served in a mission abroad (for them that would only be something you did if you served in an Order), and after lots of questions one lad said, 'And when you were in India did you make Prods?' Well, that gave me the opportunity to explain my attitude to 'Prods' – and the opposite – and I said I went out to help non-Christian people of India to understand our Christian faith and how the Lord was revealed to us in Scripture. And if they came to know Him, that was my aim, not to put labels on them!"

But according to Margaret Wilkinson, in this part of the world there is one label both Protestants and Catholics share. They are all, she says, Irish.

"I'm British *AND* Irish. Why shouldn't I be? An Englishman could be Norman or Saxon but he'd still feel English. I'm not English, I never have been. It was a foreign country to me when I went there at the age of nineteen. But I am British, and at the same time our whole Northern thing here is part of Ireland, and if you can only relate the two we can all be enriched by it. If you had a united Ireland tomorrow you wouldn't make this part fully English or fully Irish. It would continue to be the kind of Irish it is. If you touch anybody here and say they're English, they'll backfire! At the present moment the love for England is very low. We're viewed as being on the fringe and England doesn't much care for us. But the *British* thing means so much. So many died in the wars for it, and the loyalty in Ireland has been a part of the safety of England. Northern Ireland put its whole heart into the Second World War even though there was no conscription. At present, though, our value seems to have gone and there's a pretty deep feeling that England may be tiring of us. But in Ulster there is this deep, deep feeling that we have stood by her in her hour of need and though England may have no historical sense, Ulster has. And nowadays all this can be stirred up in the name of religion. That's why I've tried to help in my own situation. And that's why, although I'm not one of Dr Paisley's Free Presbyterians, I couldn't write them off as having no deep and true religious faith. But I do think they are blinded to some extent, and that in this day and age we must look for the things we have in common and strengthen them.

"We're dreadful here, I know, with our inability to accept each other, but we're still a Christian country fighting out very deep issues and, sadly, our divisions aren't caused by the people who don't go to church but by those who do! Our tragedy is that the one candle we light isn't enough – no human being can take in the immensity of it all. Look at Corrymeela – doing steadfast work – but they've only touched the surface. But it's no use saying that the little bit you can do isn't worthwhile. We've all got to try.

"I think there are testing times ahead for us. There may come a time – you saw a bit of it at the last 'Loyalist' strike – when the Protestant people will have to make up their minds in a way they haven't had to before. On the day of the strike they had to ask themselves if they were going to go to work and face the people who turned them back. There were many who turned back not from conviction but because they didn't want confrontation. But there were places where people had to stand up and be counted, and it may well be that the testing of the Protestant people is very near. And that's where people of my kind, in the mixed 'middle-class' areas, who up to now have not had to suffer, may come nearer to the experiences of the folk down on the Shankill who are facing up to the fact that their own people may turn on them. And if there are times when extreme Protestants get out on to the roads and block them with barricades then people like myself will have to decide if we just stay at home and keep out of their way or if we say 'This isn't a democratic way to go about things'. It may be that people will have to say that they are going to work, knowing that their windows will be broken and there'll be worse trouble coming. That could also extend to areas like this. I pray it won't."

Civilians in Uniform

Liz Johnston

There is a demoralizing predictability to the cycle of violence in Belfast, and after nearly two decades of it the city can reckon to have seen most of the permutations of attack and revenge. Somewhat wearily now it has come to accept them as part of the established pattern of sectarian antagonism. But the city can still spring a few grim surprises – as it did in the summer of 1986 in the wake of the Anglo-Irish Agreement. Not for the first time had the British Government devised a policy of which Ulster politicians disapproved; no, there was after all, nothing unusual about that. What was unusual, however, was the virulence with which the Loyalist factions reacted and the extraordinary turn of events their anger provoked.

For the first time the security forces – and, in particular, the Royal Ulster Constabulary, traditionally supported by those same Loyalists – became the target for Loyalist attack. In doing their job of maintaining order and imposing the law as formulated by the British Government the police were now viewed by many of their erstwhile allies as somehow conniving in the political process and tacitly responsible for upholding a policy so hated by many Ulster Protestants. A series of cold-blooded attacks on those with connections with the R.U.C. signalled an open season of calculated intimidation. Whether the intimidation succeeded can be judged, in part, by the experience of twenty-nine-year-old Liz Johnston, who became one of the early victims in this unexpected wave of Loyalist terror.

"I remember the first attack happened on a Tuesday evening just as we were going to bed. My younger sister and I were already upstairs, and my mother, who'd been

111

watching TV, was alone downstairs, tidying up before going to bed herself. All of a sudden stones were thrown through the lounge window. Stones, a half brick, and a piece of metal came flying through the window and injured my mother's arm, which later needed hospital treatment. We had no warning and we heard nothing. I dashed out straightaway but I couldn't see anyone. My sister said she heard footsteps after the attack, but because the house was in an area with lots of easy access routes you could easily make a quick getaway. At the time I put it down to vandalism and I didn't connect it with any personal attack until I rang for assistance through the 999 system and then, when help came, I realized I had been one of a number of attacks on that particular evening."

And why had Liz Johnston been singled out for special treatment? Was it perhaps because she was a high-ranking R.U.C. officer with special responsibility for mobilizing a campaign against the paramilitaries? Or was it perhaps because she headed some powerful counter-terrorist task force with inside information on outlawed organizations? Then again, could it have been that her high profile as a crime fighter in Belfast gave her a reputation which could strike fear and loathing in the men of violence? No. The reasons for her attack were more prosaic. As a part-time woman reserve constable she dared to be associated with the security forces, and the "Loyalists" were now taking their revenge. Again, as with so many people in Belfast, she was only "doing her bit" and she paid the price for it.

"I had thought of joining full-time," she says, "but I couldn't meet the height requirements. I'm only five foot three and quite petite. I have a civil service-type job in administration, so joining the R.U.C. as a part-timer was something completely different for me and it also gave me the satisfaction of knowing I was being of some help in the situation. I'm involved mostly in community relations work, like taking groups of local children from both communities to swimming classes. Sometimes I might do a bit of desk work in the station or I might help to accompany marches and bands to their destination, but mostly I'm involved with the junior swimming classes and that sort of thing. To be honest, I couldn't accept that the attack had happened. I still thought it was vandalism, and it was only after events started to deteriorate over the next few days, and the admissions were made by the various organizations, that I began to get worried.

"There was no sense in it as far as I was concerned because I wasn't involved in any decision-making of the kind the attackers disagreed with. And besides, all I was doing was five or six hours a month on community relations work — often not even in uniform! What left me feeling a bit paranoid was not knowing whether it was me or the actual uniform they were attacking. After the first attack I took a few days' leave, and because I was feeling rather uneasy I got into the habit of sleeping during the day and staying awake at night. The second attack, when it came a few days later, was much more serious.

"It was just gone midnight. My sister had gone out for the evening, my mother was dozing on the sofa, and I had just finished watching a film on the television. I had just fixed a piece of wood to the inside of the window, which was a precaution we'd taken since the first attack. We didn't put the wood up during the day as that would have attracted attention, but at night I'd put it in place once the venetian blinds were drawn. It wouldn't have stopped the window from being smashed but at least it would have prevented any injury from bricks and glass. My mother and I were both waiting for my sister to come home.

"What happened next seemed to happen in slow motion. The front door was kicked open with such a force that the inside door flew open as well, and two petrol bombs were thrown in. Nobody shouted a warning and I saw no one. All I can remember clearly is the noise — a sort of 'woosh'

113

as the petrol ignited — and the smell of the petrol which by now was setting fire to the top and the bottom of the stairs. But the most frightening thing was that some of the petrol splashed through the staircase and landed on my mother who was lying there. She came to very quickly when she heard the noise, and it was fortunate that what she was wearing was of a synthetic material which didn't actually burst into flames but just started to melt. We had to put the fires out ourselves because when one of the bombs ignited it melted the phone connection, making it impossible for us to dial 999. I used my mum's coat to pat down the flames at the bottom of the stairs, but by now the fire at the top was starting to spread along the wall. Eventually though we did get it out and then ran outside. The street was dark and there was no sign of light or life in the houses. I started to scream and shout for help, and eventually the neighbours put their lights on and phoned for the fire brigade for us. After that police assistance came very quickly and they advised us not to spend the night in the house but to move to other accommodation.

"We were too busy fighting the fire to have any immediate reaction, but my mother was badly shocked by it and had to be prescribed tranquillizers. She was in a daze for a while, wanting to know why? why? why? Then her next reaction was one of anger. I was dazed at first, too, but that gave way to feelings of paranoia. Was it something I'd done? When I finally worked out that I hadn't done anything I managed to get it into perspective. They seemed to be going for people who had loose connections with the force — parents, relatives, friends, anybody. The unfortunate thing for me was that I lived in the area where I did my part-time duty, so that's how we were known.

"A thing I found hard to take was that we lived in one of the old, established streets off the Shankill Road. I'd been born there and my mother moved in there with my father when they were married. My family was one of the oldest families in the street — afterwards when we were going through old photograph albums and scrapbooks we discovered that my grandparents had moved into that very house in 1912 after their wedding. The neighbours were very sympathetic, and they called when we were packing our things ready to move. They expressed disgust not only at the attack itself but at the fact that there were three defenceless women alone in the house.

"We had no choice but to leave the house and move to safer accommodation on the outskirts of the city. We had to go. We couldn't risk further attacks. At the time I felt very bitter and I couldn't wait to get the hell out of it because, I mean, how could you possibly trust anyone or feel secure knowing you were open to that kind of attack? It was a particularly despicable act because we lived in a two-up two-down terraced house, and if we had been upstairs at the time there would have been no possible exit because the stairs were on fire. I don't know whether the first attack was a warning but the second one certainly wasn't. It was a deliberate attempt to do physical damage.

"The intimidation hasn't succeeded, though. I can be quite stubborn and this has only made me more determined. There are others in the force who've had much greater sacrifices than I have. Of course I do have some of those feelings of paranoia. If someone phones and I don't recognize the voice I ask who it is before I admit to who I am. I find I'm very suspicious of strangers, and I've had a bit of a problem with keeping a night-light on in my room. It's ridiculous at my age, I know, but for a time after the attack I couldn't sleep alone in my room unless I had a light on. I'm hoping that fear will go away soon.

"But after all, this sort of violence isn't new in Belfast. It's been going on even before the present troubles started in 1968, and you have to get on with things. I'm an independent girl and I have to look after my mother and keep a home together. I can't afford the luxury of screaming fits and nervous breakdowns. I do my worrying in private then go out and get on with my life."

"Civilians in Uniform"

There is that same sense of cautious determination in many of the R.U.C.'s full-time serving officers. Theirs is a particularly sensitive job at present and, as I found out when I spoke to a group of them at their headquarters, they are viewing the future with unease. I was speaking to them shortly after fierce rioting had followed the police decision to ban a Loyalist Apprentice Boys' Parade in the Protestant stronghold of Portadown. The disturbance, the fury of which shocked observers and officers alike, claimed the life of one Protestant demonstrator, twenty-year-old Keith White, who was hit by a plastic bullet and spent weeks on a life-support machine before his death in the Royal Victoria Hospital in Belfast. The R.U.C. had been well used to being the object of hatred and violence by Nationalists; being jeered at and spat at by "Loyalists" armed with bricks and bottles was a frightening novelty they could have well done without. This is a collection of their reactions.

"I think at various times everybody suffers from stress. If you're sitting at home you're wondering whether someone is going to attack you, you're constantly under psychological pressure. Take the situation of the Portadown police at the moment after the Easter Monday incidents. All those officers will be looking out through their windows wondering, if a car pulls up, who's behind the wheel. Friend or foe? Now, whether you like it or not that's stress, and it affects us all in different ways. Some people might not worry excessively about it whereas others might take a week off sick and wouldn't feel fit to go on duty. The thing about R.U.C. work is that you don't differentiate between terrorism and ordinary duties. You deal with what crops up.

117

"I would say, though, that at the moment I'm more pessimistic than I have been since 1968. At the minute it would seem we're fighting on two fronts. 'Divide and conquer' is an old, hackneyed phrase but there's some truth in it. I don't think the R.U.C. can live in a community and be fighting on two fronts. We've always had a degree of 'flak' from the Loyalist areas, of course – the first policeman shot in this present campaign was shot by Protestants on the Shankill – but more recently certain things have happened which have put us into sharper conflict with that community. Bear in mind a policeman could never live in a Nationalist area – now it looks as though intimidation can't be ruled out in Unionist areas either.

"Now, I have many good Roman Catholic friends but, if you want my personal opinion, the towns in Northern Ireland which have had the greatest degree of success and kept out of trouble are the towns in which both communities have kept themselves to themselves. It's the people who come along and try to integrate people – possibly against their will – that cause the problem. For example, I was brought up in Dromore in County Down. Now, in that community they were all good neighbours but they seldom mixed as far as religion was concerned.

"My wife's father died last Christmas, and one of the visitors to the house was the local priest. The two of them had been very neighbourly. The priest used to come into my father-in-law's hairdresser's shop and have his hair cut, and they were both very friendly but never, ever would they have thought of going to each other's church. Integration can often be a self-inflicted wound. There's been a lot of artificial bringing together, and people will only really come together when they feel like it."

It is a common enough phrase in Belfast that "life is cheap". What is usually meant by that is that death has become commonplace, and the announcement that a civilian or a soldier has been shot hardly rates comment. At the R.U.C. the men feel particularly bitter at the apparent value put on their sacrifices. As one officer told me, "I know of a family whose sons had been killed and they made a point of watching the national news in the evening. The incident was not mentioned at all – and that upset them. A shooting or a bombing just rates a paragraph in the papers now."

The R.U.C. is overwhelmingly Protestant. One of the tiny handful of Roman Catholic police officers said, "Obviously there's a great sense of loss when you hear a report that a colleague has been killed. When a policeman is shot there's a tendency first of all to think whether you know him. If you don't then you can somehow shield yourself from the impact, but when it's a personal friend obviously it hits you much harder. In 1980 I was with a patrol which was ambushed. Some terrorists had taken over a house in West Belfast and we'd been called out. All of a sudden the car I was driving was filled with bullets – live rounds bouncing about everywhere – and one of my colleagues was killed outright. I was injured along with two others. Now, obviously there's a sense in which you never completely get over an incident like that but you've just got to prevent it from clouding your career or affecting your judgement."

Another officer says, "I've been to the scene of a bomb blast where I was carrying out bodies onto the street. I can remember that as if it happened yesterday – even though it was thirteen years ago. But what can you do? How do children in Beirut accept the situation? You either live with it or pack up and go. We have had some people leave but the strange thing is a lot of them come back. There has always been a terrific *esprit de corps* in the R.U.C.

"Remember, there's nothing new about all this. When I joined in 1959 there was another I.R.A. problem underway – the 1956–63 campaign. You'd have five or six years of it then comparative peace for a while, but this present campaign refuses to go. The only way we can do that is to crush the organization, just as the Mafia in America has to be smashed. But it's very difficult because they are so big and they permeate whole communities. Let's take a lad in Andersonstown [a well known Republican stronghold] who wants to join the police. He goes away to the training centre, and immediately his parents become suspect and they're ripe for intimidation from the paramilitary organizations because he has had the audacity to join a force which represents British Imperialism. From then on they will not be trusted and could be hounded out of the community. I know of one R.U.C. man who very seldom goes home for that very reason. I know a young constable who was seriously ill and who couldn't even go home to convalesce.

"And things are getting tougher now. A Protestant lad joining in East Belfast would provoke the same hostility now. Nobody in Westminster seems to learn very much. They've got to try something but they've picked a bad battleground. My feeling is that we're in reverse at the minute and accelerating all the time. We live in hope that something will take the sting out of the situation. We can't fight on two fronts; we've got to live as well as work in Belfast. We're only policemen while we're on duty. We're only civilians in uniform. At the moment the communities seem to be on a collision course.

"The pockets of hope are so small. It's like throwing a small stone into a big lake. You'll only get a tiny ripple. When the people of hope need to be knocked down then the paramilitaries on both sides will knock them down and chop them off at the knees. Think of the Peace People; they'll let them go just a wee bit but when the occasion demands it they'll put a stop to them.

"When you're talking about hope I think the one common denominator is conversion to Christ. There are people in prison who have undergone genuine conversion. Now they're never going to be the same again and they'll have something which can draw them together. Outside of that I think hope is very disjointed. I'm not sceptical at all of such conversions in prison – no more than I'm sceptical of St Paul on the road to Damascus. To me that's the only basis for hope. When these men emerge they're neither Catholic nor Protestant."

Ben Forde

Detective Constable Ben Forde has been in the force for twenty-seven years and he is one of those actively involved in finding that "common denominator" in the people he meets – from whichever side of the law they come. That characteristic, and the fact that he is, in his spare time, a writer whose experiences form the basis not only of his "Bomb City" books but also of his evangelism, have made him unique in the R.U.C. At present he is involved with a pet project of his called "Criminal Caring". The scheme is viewed with suspicion by some of his colleagues because it seems to blur what they consider is a hard-edged division between the law enforcer and the law breaker. Through his scheme Ben Forde aims to help all those who have got caught up in criminal activity, by establishing some sort of personal communication with them. Taking such a personal interest in a prisoner or a suspect is, of course, a risky undertaking for a policeman and one of which he is fully aware, but he feels it is only by forming a bond with such people that true progress can be made and the deep-seated sense of alienation can be overcome. In other respects, though, Ben Forde is a typical R.U.C. man with enough scars to prove it.

"I've been punched, kicked, spat at, chased off the streets; I've had my life threatened, I've been intimidated by telephone and I've been blown up. That was in the early seventies when we'd had warning of a bomb in Belfast. The bomb had been planted in a gas van parked in a side street in town, but we didn't know that at first. We'd been told the bomb was in one street but it turned out to be in another. I was actually standing with my back to this van

122

which contained an I.R.A. bomb. My colleague saw the window open and he put his head through and said, 'Ben, there's a funny smell'. So I opened the passenger door and I looked into the back and saw this tarpaulin cover. I lifted it and saw a bomb, and I got eight feet from it when it went off and there was virtually nothing of that van left. The blast knocked me to the ground and it was only because a concrete mixer lorry had driven between me and the van that I wasn't killed. Being such a solid vehicle it took the full force of the blast, but the lorry driver had part of his arm blown off because his arm was resting out of the open cab window. The next thing I remember was lying in hospital picking the glass out of my hair. These are some of the risks the R.U.C. faces. When you go into a known hostile area, say the Divis complex, for instance, you need a back-up of the British Army even to carry out a simple arrest. You can get bricks and bottles, petrol bombs and bullets coming your way!

"If you look at the situation today you'd say it was hopeless, and you've got to be realistic. And yet I believe God's Grace is enough to get us through. I have prayed for God to take away the violence, and although He works in individual men, still this thorn of terrorism remains. But I am conscious of a moving of people – irrespective of denominational ties – towards the Christian Church – and towards each other. There are people willing to cross the divide, as I believe I must with an I.R.A. prisoner or a U.V.F. murderer. I remember an ex-I.R.A. man and an ex-U.V.F. man in the one police station. They said, 'Ben, we're praying for you and for what you're doing.' I said, 'Look, boys, I can't be seen to be publicly identified with you for obvious reasons, because of the social and cultural groups you come from. It's dangerous for you and your families – and it's tricky for me.' But still we're praying for each other.

"I do have problems with the authorities, I must admit.

I'm not criticizing them because I believe they are wise and discerning, and they have to look at me in the same way as anybody else in security work. The work I do – one-to-one work with criminals – is a difficult job for a policeman. For instance, I've been able to work with one of the U.V.F. godfathers doing life for two murders. We've been talking about how to keep youngsters out of the organizations but obviously, given the sensitivity of that, there would be times when your colleagues would suspect your motives. I've been hauled on to the carpet, as it were, and asked why I'm visiting a prison, why I'm associating with a prisoner. My answers are plain, and most of my senior officers understand the true nature of my motives, but there have been times when other policemen in an investigation may not see me as a suitable person for that particular job. They may think I'm too sympathetic to a suspect because I have publicly acknowledged a strong caring attitude to those in crime.

"Some have said my policy is a case of too much too soon, but really I think my policy is simple. I believe that the root cause of crime is in a man's heart.

"My approach is to get alongside a man when he comes into custody – to break down the alienation keeping us apart. Now you could say that the terrorist and the policeman are alienated *de facto*, and that my vision is an idealistic one, but I believe in attacking the evil source with something stronger – the true enemy isn't the I.R.A. or the U.V.F. or the R.U.C. – and what is stronger is Jesus Christ. Now there's no point in me saying that unless I'm prepared to go alongside a murderer and say, 'You haven't got peace, my friend. The peace I give unto you is not the peace the I.R.A. gives you, or the Anglo-Irish Agreement gives you. My peace is a deep personal one that comes through faith in Jesus Christ.'

"Let me give you an example of how I might go about it. Here is my own Bible; it's marked '28.2.85, 9 R.U.C.' at

124

Psalm 91. It refers to the nine R.U.C. officers murdered in Newry. Now, how do I link all this together? Well, I was sitting interviewing a man arrested in connection with those nine murders, and whenever I went into the interview room I gave him my identity. The first time he said, 'Would you be the man that wrote the book?' Right, where do you go from there? Well, as a matter of fact we didn't go anywhere for he reserved his right to remain silent for seven days. But bear in mind that on average I spoke to him for something like six hours a day in, say, three two-hour interviews (even though he never spoke a word). The charges against him which were based on the evidence of a 'supergrass' were subsequently withdrawn and he got off. But what does that man think today? He'll be left with the impression of seven days with me and several other detectives. All I'm saying is that I had to communicate with him. I would have read him portions of books, I would have talked through with him the experiences of the widows and orphans. We could have talked about politics, about boundaries, and I would have told him that I don't believe God made the boundaries and I would have told him that I don't believe God made the boundaries of Ireland to be fought over.

"Of course the sessions differ. If you go to any solid terrorist man he'll tell you how he was ill-treated, tortured, degraded and so on. Indeed I have also been accused of a form of mental brainwashing, and I have been the subject of an Amnesty International report. There have been complaints of beating and torture – none of which I have ever done.

"The longest time I have spoken would be five or six hours. You work harder if you feel you're getting somewhere. I don't have the same resilience as I did when I was younger. A man gets tired after investigating so many murders, and I have to say I'm prone to weakness, to depression and to the feelings of other people. And I thank the Lord that I'm still sensitive to those feelings because it means I'm not immune to the needs of the prisoners or the victims. And I have to keep both in mind. If you're down, it's hard to get up. And I think it's harder in many cases for the criminal. That's when I think I can help – if he's responsibly minded, that is – you can only help those who feel a need for help. Of course, it's not the same with all criminals. If you get one who doesn't give a damn about what he's done there's very little you can do. Then there's a sense of hopelessness, of worthlessness, of job frustration such as you can barely describe, when you get suspects wanted for murder answering sarcastically and when you just can't get through the hatred and the evil. Even in your failure, though, you can learn.

"I remember visiting a police widow one time. Her late husband had been a police inspector who had been murdered, and the widow had written to the man who had murdered him. Her house overlooked the Maze Prison. It was a very gloomy night and the orange lights surrounding the Maze were shining brightly. I made some comment about how black it was out there and she said to me, 'The darker the night, the brighter the light'. Now that's a nice thing to say, but sometimes when you're with an evil person it's not always so, for you come home dark yourself and you say, 'Lord, help!' – But I believe when you cry out like that in your weakness the God of all comfort comes alongside you and can help you, like the police widow, come through the valley of deep grief.

"Now, I think it's because of experiences like that that I can be of practical help to the people I meet. I can understand their deeper grief, their suicidal tendencies, their wanting to opt out of life or wanting to emigrate. I think I can then come alongside them and, through my experiences and the message of the Gospel, encourage them. There's no reason why you can't help a man practically by, say, buying him a meal, supporting him in prison, pro-

126

viding for him or putting him in touch with someone who will if you're prevented from doing so because of your position. Those are the weapons which will eventually end this war in Ulster.

"I do feel quite alone in my work. Now I do not want to sound uncharitable to the R.U.C. because they have never stood in the way of my books, and I got a lot of help and useful suggestions from them, but in my work at present I feel quite alone. In many ways I'm crying out for support, but I know that self-pity is dangerous so I accept the lonely ministry I'm in and I carry on. I do feel that many of my colleagues think my Christian charity to murderers and criminals is misplaced. I must do justice to the authorities though, because they may well know more than I do in this respect. Even so, in the past I have been forbidden to go to every prison in this land by a senior police officer. I hold no personal animosity to the man at all because I realize I have to uphold the good name of the force. I'm allowed to go in my own time, but even when I do go in my own time, I've got a problem – and this is very sensitive. In one case, for instance, although I was allowed to go inside the prison it was only on condition I went in through the general public entrance. That is, I would have to meet the wives and the children of all those bigoted camps and they would see me. Now, maybe my faith is not strong enough but my commonsense and Christian judgement would say I must not go that way because I could create a scene leading to violence; I could be seized or murdered, a prison officer could be injured, a civilian could be injured and I would bring the whole name of the R.U.C. into disrepute because of my Christian ministry. So I have to accept limitations. But there are other ways of communicating; for example, by letter writing. And here I have every co-operation from the prison service. But you must do it in your own time.

"Most of those that know me give me a bit of friendly banter but there are others who question my motives.

Some think I'm making a fortune out of my books (which I'm not), some see me as sincere, and others see me as sincerely wrong and dangerous as far as my law enforcement is concerned. Sometimes, I wish I'd gained a promotion or two but that's just my personal ego. Then again I'm thankful I didn't – at least I can't go down any further, other than out! Otherwise I just carry on as a detective constable, a plain-clothes Christian policeman.

"I'm not completely on my own and I do get some encouragement and, of course, the support of a loving family and friends. But I can honestly say that one of the chaps who's helping me most is a man doing time for murder. Where I have received no help from any official source, it's through him that I've been encouraged morally, spiritually and practically. Both of us have a vision. I can see how he got into wrong and how other young paramilitaries get into wrong and he, in his turn, can see the wrongs of the interviewing officers. Here we have a unique situation and nobody wants to know. He could see the wrongs in various forms of policing – now, again, the fact that I listen to him may be why I'm seen as a danger to authority. Let me make it clear, though, that I'm proud to be a policeman. A crime is a crime and I get on with it. I have had many encouraging letters from other prisoners too, and I would love to get as many letters from policemen but I don't get them.

"I don't want to sound like a unique policeman in the R.U.C. but I have been around for a long time – at the nitty gritty end of it – and the fact that I'm not officer material or up there in management means I've been down here among it all probably for longer than any other policeman. I feel our police force is more alienated today than ever it was. And that's not healthy – look at Portadown. I've seen murder everywhere and I've seen crime everywhere. I've seen evil minds and evil attitudes at work in the places I've served, whether in Andersonstown or Belfast City centre.

And all the time I've found myself not preaching but sharing my faith, and in the contact I had with criminals saying, 'Be careful that your experience of evil doesn't destroy you because that's a slower death than the man killed by a bomb.' That's part of my role as a policeman and as a peace officer."

West Belfast

Falls

"It was about one o'clock in the morning when the bomb went off in the church. I was in bed in the presbytery next door. First of all I felt a shock wave. I had the impression in the whole of my brain that something was going wrong with me, as if I was going to faint. It seemed to last for a few seconds, this strange sensation that my mind was going funny, and then the next thing I heard was the explosion. It was quite a sizeable bomb packed into a gas cylinder. I think the congregation sort of expected something like this because we were in a vulnerable area and there had been some tension in the air, but it was still disappointing to see someone come along and wreck what you're so proud of. We'd put so much hard work into raising the three quarters of a million pounds we needed for a new church, and in a couple of seconds there it was in ruins."

Such was the experience four years ago of Father Sean Connolly. The "vulnerable" area he talks of is on the Cavehill Road to the north of the city, where proposals to build the Church of the Resurrection had met "Protestant" opposition. There had been objections at the planning stage, followed by petitions, public meetings and even road blocks, but because the Catholic population was on the increase in that part of town and the existing two churches could no longer cope, a third church was needed. There was good reason, says Father Connolly, why the population was increasing; it was a peaceful, residential area and a desirable mixed part of town to move to. True, there had been kneecappings and assassinations from time to time, but by and large it was an area well removed from the large public housing estates where much of the trouble

133

is focused. It was all a long way from Father Connolly's position now as one of the priests in charge at the Divis complex of flats on the Falls Road. This is the classic Belfast "ghetto", where no mix of denominations is thought possible or desirable. Is Father Connolly happier here in the ghetto than he was in the suburbs?

"You have a different set of problems to deal with. At least here our windows don't get broken regularly, the church isn't stoned twice a week, and I don't get people shouting obscenities at me as some of the 'Loyalists' did up along the Antrim Road, but life here in the Divis is hard. Until you've been here a while, as I have, you've no idea what it's like. To be honest, I find it quite a trial. The people here are very poor and there's a sort of desperation in the air. You'd love to be able to lift them out of these awful housing conditions but you know it's going to take a long, hard slog. The only answer is to pull them down and replace them with decent housing."

So far the complaint may echo that made earlier by Pat Buckley, but there the similarity between the two men ends. Father Connolly is no extrovert, no showman, no maverick. He would not make the news with dramatic gestures. He is an ordinary, unassuming parish priest in the mainstream of Catholic ministry.

"You have army foot patrols going round twice a day, and the constant presence of the soldiers reminds you of the trouble you'd like to forget. And then there's the occasional raid, when the place is flooded with army and police jeeps and soldiers looking out at every corner. At moments like that you'll look out of the presbytery here and know that some poor family is at the centre of it. They may have been involved in some trouble or they may be completely innocent. All you have to do is drop somebody's name to the authorities if you've got something against them, and they're liable to come in and pull the place apart. I've seen that a few times; their furniture

134

ripped up, the panelling in their homes pulled apart just maybe because somebody has a grudge.

"We've a combination of hoods and paramilitaries (of various Republican strains) and the hoods sometimes seem to do what they like. The hoods are straightforward criminals, teenagers mostly, and they're quite powerful. They can thumb their noses at near enough anybody. The paramilitaries can't really control them. Sure, a few guys have been kneecapped, and once there was a mishap when they tried to punish someone and accidentally shot him dead, but that's bad publicity for them because when a fellah's shot his family and relations are up in arms. The hoods openly bring cars in here and delight in it. I've seen delivery vans pulling up and boys taking parcels out of them and then running off. They're quite barefaced about it, so there's not much you can do except challenge them. I have reported some of them to the police and we've retrieved the odd car, but then again the police are afraid to come here. If I report a stolen car the police may come along, look at it and drive past, worried that it might be booby-trapped. There have been days which have seen me watching a car for a full twelve hours – well, you know, I've other things to do! I'd love to see some sort of law and order, and I think most people in here would be of the same mind, but they can't go against the paramilitaries and they can't bring in the R.U.C. or they're going to be molested as police-lovers. The only way you will get away from it is when there's a rising of public opinion and people say they'll have to get rid of it themselves. Now and again you feel that's coming.

"We don't have any grand scheme which you could say is bringing great hope, but we've all sorts of little schemes which we trust are bringing people away from the violence. For instance, in our youth centre we've started a boxing club to appeal to the 'hard-man' element, the unclubbable element round here; we've started an A.C.E. scheme to get unemployed kids learning a trade or something. Male unemployment is around the eighty per cent mark, it could be going on for ninety per cent, although there's a bit more for the women who can get shop assistants' jobs or part-time work cleaning in the hospital.

"People are generally browned off with the violence. It just adds to the whole melancholy that invades the place. We are a depressed people in here and we're very conscious of it – you hear it from people as you go around. For instance, in Holy Week of 1985 we had a bomb go off just outside here. In fact, I'd passed by it ten minutes earlier. I was just sitting down to take my lunch when it went off, and when I got to the window all I could see was dust and two or three soldiers going berserk shouting at one another. At that stage people were beginning to pour out of the flats, and as the dust was settling I caught a glimpse of clothes among the rubble. I reckoned it was a soldier so I told one of the other priests who was standing outside to run along there quickly. He anointed the young soldier – a Catholic fellah as it turned out – and gave him the last rites. We also run a dinner club for the local 'winos', and a few of them caught the blast as they were ambling by. They were taken off to hospital but it was only the soldier who died. The bomb was in a shed and detonated from one of the flats by means of a wire running up the side of the building. The poor wee lad had no chance because he was standing right in front of it. But the point is that the bomb was left in a very public place – women and children had been walking past it – and the people here were disgusted by the whole thing. There was a lot of opposition to it but I don't suppose it changed much. Most of the folk here are decent people held to ransom by the lawlessness."

One thing that does not affect the Divis is sectarianism. The flats are a hundred per cent Catholic and there is no contact with the Protestants just half a mile away. It is this very quality of isolation, of being a people set apart, that helps to propagate a lot of the myths. Fear and ignorance have long fed on each other. Father Connolly will tell you that most people here do not hate the Protestants on the Shankill, that their housing and employment chances are the same, but he adds that whenever the violence starts up people are forced into their corners and will automatically defend their own. And, of course, memories are no shorter in the Divis than they are elsewhere in Belfast, as Father Connolly explains.

"This was the first place to come under attack from the 'B' Specials in 1969. They and the R.U.C. fired into the flats with Browning machine guns mounted on Land-Rovers, and killed a young lad as he lay there in his bed. People don't forget that, and that's one of the reasons the police aren't welcome even today. At the time this parish stretched further afield towards the Shankill, and night after night Catholic streets would be burnt out by the Protestants, and the police didn't seem to be giving them any help at all. They don't forget that it was Protestant neighbours who pointed them out to the mobs, and that the police weren't so quick at preventing the mob from burning them out of their homes.

"You've got lots of people in the Divis today who lost all their possessions at that time. One woman, for example, came out of her house with nothing more than her night-dress, and finished up living in a garage for six months until she and her family were found a flat to live in over here. And that woman's been scared ever since – she's had bad health and nervous breakdowns through having lost her confidence in people. She can tell you the person who pointed them out to the mob – he's since been shot dead, so they tell me – he was the boy who used to deliver the papers to them every day, but he pointed the finger because they used to get the Irish newspapers. And the mob bombed them out and left them with nothing. A lot of the bitterness may have gone but it's not forgotten and it's easily played on.

"We have very good people here but the troubles have had

a demoralizing effect. The community spirit that there was in the old streets has gone, and these flats have never succeeded in regenerating it. They're rabbit warrens, really. For example, the sleeping accommodation is positioned underneath these echoing walkways (if a dog barks at night it's like a lion roaring) and the slightest noise in the evening wakes people up and puts a lot of stress on them. If it's the hoods creating a disturbance it takes a brave person to go out and tackle them and then risk broken windows at two or three in the morning. But some of the time it's just ordinary kids playing out late. I suppose you could say that the parents should keep them indoors and not let them out. The trouble is that they have so little as it is that letting them play out is a way of indulging them. There's not much parents can do in the way of 'spoiling' their children with toys and presents, because they just don't have the money; letting them run around a bit is a way of making up for what they lack.

"All the Church can do is stand by these people and represent them when they need it. I think we've been more successful than we've been given credit for – simply because we don't go out in public and claim the credit. As long as it's done for the good of the folks here we don't mind who claims the glory. That's the vision we have of things, and it's one shared by a lot of the people here. Good-will is kept suppressed by the fact that so many of them are so vulnerable, but we've a core of good men and women who are working for the future. You know, the troubles have been a testing time; they've sorted out the strong believers from the wishy-washy ones, and we're left with a lot of people who are all the stronger for it. That's where our hope is."

123 Springhill Avenue

It was bitterly cold on the April night I first visited 123 Springhill Avenue – from the outside an ordinary enough maisonette looking rather bleak in the dark night, and the howling wind beneath an unexpected flurry of spring snowflakes. So very commonplace did it look that the taxi driver drove past it twice and eventually had to ask for directions himself in the labyrinthine streets of the Roman Catholic Ballymurphy estate in West Belfast.

Several times I had stayed with a family on the estate and knew well enough that Ballymurphy was unremarkable by day – noisy, full of children, with that featureless semi-detached look of any other slightly run-down council estate on the mainland, but with the outer bleakness re-deemed by the warmth and hospitality of the people I had met. But by night a sodden Irish tricolour flailing loudly from an improvised flagpole in an upstairs bedroom, and the street names in English and in Gaelic, seemed to generate an unexpected shade of unease in this nocturnal English visitor – especially as the cab had deposited him among a large crowd of unsmiling youths in the ill-lit streets at the heart of the estate. It was a momentary disquiet dispelled as soon as I entered the house. And soon it became clear that what was an ordinary council house on the outside was in every other respect quite extraordinary. Here was a school and meeting house; a debating club and a home from home; a college and a welfare centre; a place of learning and of culture. It "belongs" to Father Des Wilson, priest, newspaper columnist, community politician and seasoned observer of the Northern Irish scene, a man who decided to open up his own home in 1974 to act as a focus for fellow feeling in what was a deprived and, at the time, particularly troubled part of the city. It is an example of how ordinary people can change their own lives; an example of what Belfast is good at – taking a personal stake in its future, knowing what it wants and working for it, putting its own unique handprint on its destiny. Joe Reid, a "graduate" and staff member of this "college for life" told me what the house stands for.

"An acceptance of human beings as they are – not as you think they should be. An attempt to help people realize the dignity they were born with. In the daytime we've got a dozen or so children on our roll. They're normally thirteen to sixteen-year-olds who don't fit into ordinary schools and who react by playing truant. We've got all sorts of other people, too, who might drop in casually for basic English classes and literacy schemes. Others might want advice on housing or social security. They might use our phone service for getting details of solicitors or tenants' groups or whatever. We have two theatre groups and discussion classes. Speakers discuss philosophy and religion, and then the points raised will be open for general debate. The talk is good, the company is good."

So far it may seem a small-scale undertaking like many another community centre. It would, however, be mistaken to think that. In scope and quality 123 Springhill is in a category of its own, as Joe Reid and another "staffer" there, Noelle Ryan, will tell you.

"We're not talking about just a handful coming through this place. We're talking about hundreds of people a week coming in here. People from all professions, all shades of politics, Catholic and Protestant – a wealth of talent in all shapes and sizes. We have one of the most eminent psychologists in Northern Ireland who teaches O and A Level classes here. We have ex-Queen's lecturers giving public talks in the evenings, specialist academics on Irish Literature. We have the whole critics' circle up here –

poets, playwrights,. artists — and a complete spectrum of 'visiting lecturers'."

It is a place of culture indeed, a place where the phrase "community education" (for which it provides a shining model) seems at once perfect and strangely inadequate. It is a place, quite simply, of education, a place of enlightenment.

If it represents that pool of light, though, how could it be, I wondered, that I had sensed a fleeting whiff of unease outside in the darkness?

"It's wise to be afraid round here", said Joe. "A lot of people are afraid round here once nightfall comes. I mean, when I see dusk I'm like a farmer gathering up his sheep. I'm afraid at 2.30 in the morning, say, if I come home from somewhere and meet a British Army foot patrol in an alley. The danger's being 'lifted' and your family not knowing about it, or getting a hiding or being arrested. Fear's a good means of survival. Mind you, I'm past the danger age now at thirty-eight but if you're eighteen, nineteen or twenty you're potentially dangerous to them. For example, if you'd been here an hour earlier you wouldn't have moved for foot patrols." That I could corroborate from past experience. I well remembered the couple of dozen soldiers, the Army jeeps, and the two helicopters circling overhead with searchlights blazing down on, among others, the house where I was staying — the whole commotion, incidentally, keeping awake the fifteen-year-old daughter of my hosts as she prepared, unsuccessfully, to get a good night's rest before her music exam the next day. The fear, however, as Joe suggested in his description of the twenty-year-olds, is not one-sided. The Army fears the threat from the shadows as much as the youngsters fear harrassment from the Army or assassination by Protestant groups. And fear has a habit of generating itself.

"A lot of people make themselves housebound," says Joe, "and what this place does is to give them the opportunity to widen their horizons. It's a place where people of all ages can express their opinions freely and feel secure. Now, from what I've said, you may feel it's just a cocoon, keeping people sheltered and shielded, and I suppose in many ways it is, because in a place like this a cocoon is exactly what's needed for some people, so that they can develop into themselves without any fear.

"When we started there was no facility for school refusers so we just started one up ourselves. It came about when some parents made it clear that however much they tried to get their kids to school they just refused to go. They were at the end of their tether because they really cared about their children, but still they played truant. So we opened our doors here. It started informally but gradually the word spread and it now plays a vital role. The kids we get might be troublemakers elsewhere, but when they get here they calm down. We had a girl here who had been told she was beyond education, but it was really because her energy and her vitality didn't fit in. After a fortnight things settled down."

It is something with which Joe himself instinctively sympathizes. He was, as he puts it, "turfed out" of a school run by Christian Brothers at the age of twelve, for hitting a teacher. At his next school his "name" for being a hard boy preceded him but he overcame it and conformed, eventually gaining nine O levels and leaving school at fifteen. Shortly after that, he says, he went for an interview for a technical job at a firm in Belfast. His story is a familiar one to many a Catholic in the city.

"They asked me to do a test and then they asked me my school qualifications. The test went OK, and a guy on the interview panel came out behind me and said, 'By rights, son, the job should be yours but you'd better apply to another firm.' I asked him why and he said, 'You kick with the wrong foot!' (i.e. you're a Catholic). After that I put in fifty applications or more (my mother can tell you better) for jobs and apprenticeships, and I got nowhere. Then I hit on the idea of changing my address from 'The Falls Road' to 'Off the Grosvenor Road' (which is a mixed area) and I got an interview. I didn't get the job, of course, because as soon as I told them what school I'd been to they knew — and that was that."

Joe did get a number of jobs eventually — in a book wholesaler's and then as a painter and decorator but, as he explains, "I've never had a job long enough to remember what redundancy's like. The work got really bad in the late 1970s and now eighty to ninety per cent of heads of household are unemployed on Ballymurphy." Two years ago, however, Joe took A levels after somewhat reluctantly being "coaxed" into 123 Springhill by his wife. He studied at the Polytechnic and now, along with five other people in the house, is doing an honours degree at the university.

But all the varied success stories do not mask the difficulties they had in the early days in developing the house as a school.

"There was a lot of hassle", says Joe, "from the education welfare officers. People were told their allowances would be cut off if they sent their kids here. People were threatened with court. They wouldn't have hassled them if they'd let their kids roam the streets, of course! When they came here they were coming to an 'uncontrolled' school and that wasn't on! But we've no desire to fragment the education system. We don't want to replace it, we want to complement it with what we have.

"We have a shared ethos in this house — it isn't a question of it being imparted by someone in authority. A lot of the kids here have been shouted at for most of their school lives, their self-image has been bruised and they've been damaged. After a while here, though, they seem to blossom, their heads come up and it's a joy to see them. Nobody ever lays blame here. We don't say, 'Your problems are deprivation, bad housing, unemployment or this institution or that institution', we just accept people as they come to us, treat them with dignity and move forward with a sense of shared responsibility to each other.

"We had a girl in here whose father had been shot by the British Army. She had a lot of problems and was disruptive even here in the house. It got so bad that someone suggested that because her presence was interrupting everybody else she should go. But Desmond [Father Des Wilson, the founder] believes that if the school removes a child like that then nobody learns from the situation. Whereas if everybody makes an effort to cope with it – and maybe suffers somewhat in the process – perhaps everybody will come through it and learn from it. Well, we all stuck with her and that girl's a tremendous help to us now – helping in every way, dealing with all sorts of people, having time for everybody. She's a happily married woman now who is part of the backbone of this place.

"You see, once you accept that everybody is redeemed by Christ in the temple of the Holy Spirit then you have to look at people in a totally fresh light. If there's a need for a place like this anywhere else in Belfast we'll be ready to give whoever wants it the benefit of our experience. And if there's a need for it on the Shankill we'll help them there, too."

Healing the Wounds

(i) Clonard

"Rebuilding bridges between the two peoples is a slow process and none of us has any grand project. It's like the break up of a marriage – there's no magic formula, no easy solution. By all the natural laws the people here in West Befast – Protestant and Catholic – are the same folk. They've answered the factory hooters for generation after generation, and in normal circumstances they would have been very close to each other. But the split has come and now, with a war going on as well, healing the division is difficult indeed."

The words of Father Gerry Reynolds, one of the eighteen Redemptorists at the Clonard Monastery just off the Falls Road and a few hundred yards away from the Peace Line separating the two communities. Walk up the road a little, then through a tiny gateway in the wall, and you are in the Shankill. One wall dividing two cultures. For most Protestants on the Shankill Father Reynolds' native church would have all the exotic appeal of Notre Dame or Chartres, so far removed is it from their everyday experience. Similarly, for most Catholics a walk through the narrow gate to the Shankill a few hundred yards away would have the dimensions of a great adventure.

"What I've tried to do", says Father Reynolds, "is to form some sort of fellowship between the clergy of both sides. We managed to bring Presbyterian, Methodist and Church of Ireland clergy from across the way into the monastery with priests from this side, and we've met several times since we began three years ago. Some people have said that it's the clergy itself which has perpetuated the divide but I don't look at it like that. Who is to decide guilt but the Almighty? The Church isn't in the business of bringing condemnation. There's been far too much of that. I mean, who are the guilty ones? The prisoners in Long Kesh who have, out of sheer frustration, taken guns into their hands? Or the people who have violence in their hearts and superiority over the ordinary people here? Violence is a terrible and uncontrollable thing, but when you look at the seeds which produce the crop you realize they've been sown by many, many people – and not just by those with the guns and bombs. One day lots of folk will find themselves in the courtroom to answer for what has happened here. In the meantime all the Church can do is bring the compassion of Christ.

"The churches are part of the people and consequently have all their weaknesses as well. They too are affected by the tribalism of things. It's Good Friday tomorrow and the combined churches of the Shankill will be celebrating at Woodvale Park while we do the same here in the Falls, and we'll both be celebrating the fact that we have redemption and new life through the death of Christ, and yet we'll be finding it so hard to make that new life visible, to transform it into an everyday reality in the city. But you work on in hope, putting your trust in ordinary people.

"I remember going over to the Shankill last July with some Swiss friends. We went through the gate in the wall and got chatting to three old ladies there, Dorothy, Elizabeth and Margaret. I mentioned to one of them that I wasn't Swiss myself but was in fact a very near neighbour of theirs from the monastery, and I added that I felt rather nervous. 'Oh, never be nervous', she said. 'Never be afraid. Just put your trust in God and do the things which are right.' And I must say that simple, strong word has always been an encouragement to me to press on. You feel there might just be progress after all. The lady told me she was no stranger to Clonard, that she regularly came to inter-church services during the Week of Prayer for Christian Unity, then she whispered to me, 'But I've never told the other two that I do.' There is a lot going on under the surface of things in Belfast.

"Fear is the most crippling thing operating in the lives of people round here. Only last January we were developing some contact between a dozen or so fourteen-year-olds – just a small scheme – bringing together Protestant and Catholic lads in the YMCA to play and chat in the hope that they would carry on meeting. They did so for a while, then the parents asked me not to continue because they were afraid of what might happen if they carried on associating with Catholics.

"Is it religion keeping us apart? I think not. True religion does not divide. It passes no judgement. It puts the onus on us to accept each other with the same unconditional love with which we ourselves are accepted by our Saviour. Its purpose is to unite people, but because it searches the heart it will also drive some away – those who seek power, prestige, and domination over others. The sectarianism which says, 'I will not accept you until you accept my formulation of the truth', is the force that cuts people off from each other. Where is the unconditional love there? I remember a short while ago the visit by Cardinal Suenens to the Cathedral. I was there while the protesters inside and outside were shouting. At one point the Cardinal said, by way of calming them down, 'My dear brothers and sisters'. And a man next to me in a clerical collar stood up on his seat and shouted out, 'You're no brother of mine!' Why can we not be accepted as brothers in Christ?

"This doctrine of limited atonement – that Christ only dies for the elect and isn't the head of the *whole* human race – becomes a real problem which separates people. This feeling that only when you are 'saved' can you be accepted as a brother in Christ, otherwise you are one of the children of wrath – this is destructive of ordinary, human relationships. I would not for one moment say that these people are not Christians – many of them are deeply pious men and women – but I would have to say they are Christians in error over their perception of the Catholic Church.

"We'll never be one unless we love one another, and we'll never love one another unless we know one another, so what we are doing here is giving people the opportunity to experience worship of the one God with other churches. Many of our services are open but people have to be helped and shown the way. That's where the clerical leadership comes in, I suppose. Was it Burke who said, 'All you need for the triumph of evil is for good men to do nothing'? That's our principle here – to go on trying. I'm not a prophet so I don't know if we're making any breakthrough. All I know is that I'll keep on doing it until I die, so I suppose that must mean I'm hopeful, mustn't it? Sure, we won't have the new world in the morning but it will be small attempts at love and understanding which will eventually usher in the new day."

(ii) Royal Victoria Hospital

"We have wounded soldiers and wounded terrorists here; Protestants and Catholics whose flesh is torn, and we can only look after them by accepting their common humanity and proceeding on that basis. That's a very suspect thing to do in Northern Ireland."

We end where we began, in the casualty unit of the Royal Victoria Hospital with Mr William Rutherford, who since the opening words of the first chapter were written down has now retired after twenty years in the front line.

"We've not always been seen as neutral ground up here", he says. "People have feared a religious or a political bias in the system. The extreme Protestant would see a lot of people on the staff as having brothers or fathers in jail for terrorism, and so could not put his trust in the work we do. On the other hand the Nationalists might see it as a place manipulated by the Establishment for its own ends, say as a place to use medical records as means for gathering information for security purposes. It is very unpleasant becoming the focus for argument because it's inclined to polarize the staff, who otherwise get on perfectly well together as a close-knit team. I'm sure there'd be people who'd look on me as being a very queer person for saying that – a very unsound Protestant! I'm both an Ulster Scot and an Irishman, and I can't deny both things but some people are very hurt to hear me say it.

"We ignore all the borders here, all the divisions. The patient is just a patient here – no matter what has happened. Any judgements are held back in abeyance while you get on with the job of giving him his transfusion, taking his X-ray, recording the details. If you're a pedestrian knocked down by a car I can't afford to get uptight about whether motorists are driving dangerously; I have to get on with the task of patching you up. Nor can you worry about your philosophical attitude to the problem of violence. You proceed as if the patient had no feelings and you had no feelings, and you solve problems the way you would solve a crossword puzzle. Whether violence is excusable or understandable or inevitable or whatever is something you can work out afterwards – in the meantime there are more urgent matters on hand.

"I think only once can I remember, as it were, breaking the rule. We'd had a bomb go off in town with lots of casualties, and a child in a tiny ski-suit was brought in. The child was so small, and as the parents carried it in, dead in their arms, you couldn't help but be aware of the shock and the outrage – even while all the work was going on. Doctors are trained to separate emotion from expertise but at that point I had an instant emotional reaction – one of sadness more than anything else, pity for the parents.

"Being close to the violence has propelled me into all sorts of searches for understanding. It would be very neat and simple to be a pacifist. I think you have to realize how and why violence comes about, that people's emotions will, when pressed beyond a certain point, lead them to violence. And that happens on both sides. I might feel that in certain situations the only honest recourse I had to defend my family was to fight for them. I think the root cause of the violence is the balance of power. Adjustments have to be made, and people who have the power find it very painful to give it up.

"Although I hate it all and long for a resolution I don't think that will come without there being more violence, and I think it will be partly the awfulness of the violence that will bring people to the negotiating table ready to bargain seriously. But the violence is a very complicated issue, stemming undoubtedly in part from the system and the state. Part of the violence and the injustice is between those who have money, power, and jobs, and those who are totally excluded from all those things. And I'm not sure you can totally understand the problems here without examining that aspect of it all as well as the Protestant/ Catholic issue, because part of the injustice which is causing the whole situation to fester is the existence of these great groups of people who are left watching the TV pictures of all the wonderful things life has to offer but which they will never enjoy.

"The funny thing is, though, that there is far more encounter today between Protestant and Catholic and between Nationalist and Unionist than there ever was before. Right enough, it's a minority movement, but it's a far bigger minority than it was in '68, say. In the religious sense, when you realize that the things that unite you are more profound than what divides you you can make progress, and the gains made are all the more valuable for being achieved in situations which are quite extraordinary. I've been a member of the Corrymeela Community, for example, since before the troubles, and although there are only something like a hundred and fifty members, their friends and associates run into thousands and the influence they have is out of all proportion to their numbers. The incident which sparked off the Peace Movement arrived in our department, and from then on I was involved in many of the marches myself. What it did demonstrate − even though the big popular thing came and went − was that ordinary people in tough working-class areas can be part of a big movement in a genuine way. And that's what's needed: political activity at the highest level underpinned by the good faith and good will of the people at large. As to whether there are enough of them, you can only work on without the answer."

A gloomy indication of the amount of good will available, however, came to Dr Robert Gray a few years ago, when as consultant anaesthetist in the intensive care unit he opened his doors one Saturday afternoon to five new patients, who between them were to lose ten limbs as a result of a bomb which had exploded without warning in a café. At about the same time, he recalls, a sixth patient was admitted with bullet wounds. He had been shot by the Army while placing a bomb outside a shop. "I often mused in my own mind", says Dr Gray, "how spending three weeks in an atmosphere of misery and mutilation would affect the lad. One of the girls had lost both legs up to the thigh, and an arm, and her sister was partly blinded and had lost both legs. He knew how they had come to be there but it clearly had no effect on him whatsoever, because shortly after he'd been released from prison I read that he had been caught putting a bomb outside a supermarket. They may realize the tragedy they've caused later on in their lives, but when they're young they don't seem to have a clue. A lot of the people we see in here who've been injured while involved in some disturbance are between eighteen and twenty years old. Once a disturbance starts you've no shortage of young people eager to take part."

One such youngster in the ward as we spoke was Keith White – at the time the latest victim of a security forces' plastic bullet fired in the Protestant riot in Portadown. The Loyalist reaction to the Anglo-Irish Agreement was by now well under way, and Keith White paid the price for, as people in Northern Ireland are apt to say, "being in the wrong place at the wrong time". As we spoke Dr Gray could hold out little hope for him because of the brain damage the bullet had caused. He died shortly afterwards.

"I try to be as sympathetic to relatives as I can. I've had people brought in blown up by bombs and blown up making bombs. It's not my job to start moralizing to them, telling them the rights and wrongs of what they've done when they're dangerously and desperately ill. I'm there to pick up the pieces. But you can't, at times, help feel a bitter shame at being a member of a community where this sort of thing could happen."

Dr Gray, incidentally, was described to me by Pearl McKeown, the mother of Karen who herself was looked after by him, as "a good Christian man". He shrugged off the title modestly, saying with some weariness that in Belfast all too often "a good Christian man" was a contradiction in terms. All too often, he said, Christian meant a rather pious and self-centred fanaticism. "I'm not decrying the real Christians," he said after a pause, "it's just that the genuine article's rather a rare commodity."

To which his colleague, Mr Rutherford, added, "If your faith is important to you you have to believe that the affairs of this world are in the hands of God and that the things that look weak are actually profoundly strong. You have to believe that the small signs of progress and hope are far more tenacious than they look – even when the evidence of your eyes is not terribly persuasive."

Postscript

I said at the beginning that this book represents an outsider's view, the record of yet another visitor to an endlessly fascinating city. It is interesting to note that in arriving at the stories contained here I had to reject many more. And why? Not because they were uninteresting or unrepresentative but because they had been heard before. How many times did I during my trips to Belfast hit on a man or a woman whose story would enthral any writer but who, twenty minutes into some riveting tale, would add, "But it's all written in a book by So-and-So. You can read it for yourself there"? For a time it seemed as if everyone in Belfast were writing a book! It made the job of editing any collection a difficult one but it was, so I realized afterwards, only to be expected in a place where there is, quite simply, so much to say, a place where the old newspaper phrase "All human life is there" is not a boast but a fact.

The city's tragedy (and surely this is the appropriate word) is that its strengths spring directly from its weaknesses, that the warmth and the welcome and the friendliness shine all the more clearly against the city's backdrop of cruelty. Many, many people told me that they have the distinct impression that nobody, least of all England, cares about them, and that in feeling abandoned by those outside they have been thrown back on their own qualities and resources. Many of the things we on the mainland enjoy are denied to whole sections of Belfast's population. Many people in the city have nothing, and if you have nothing there is a case for saying you have everything. At the very least, because things cannot get

worse, you have freedom to go whichever way you choose:
the freedom to create your own hope and the freedom to
destroy what little you have. In Belfast it means the
freedom to do good by performing acts of impressive
self-sacrifice, or to do harm by causing pain in deliberate
and sometimes chilling ways.

On the subject of pain let me conclude with a personal
recollection, an ironical and, I know, faintly ridiculous
counterpoint to Belfast's violence. Shortly after completing
the final section of the book set in the Royal Victoria
Hospital I was involved in an accident myself. Nothing
serious – I slipped and broke a finger, my little finger in
fact. The top half-inch of the tip of my left hand's little
finger, to be precise. Now was that a wound? Surely,
injuries to the human body do not come more trivial than
that. And yet it hurt like Hell. I could not sleep that night
for the pain. The tip of one little finger. How absurd! With
that minor gauge to potential levels of pain I could not help
but wonder what a faceful of glass, what burning hair,
what shattered knees must feel like. Let alone a hole in the
thigh as big as a soup plate, or the swift explosive removal
of an arm while still in its sleeve.

And yet for all that, Belfast is a place to return to, and
despite its reputation I know few people who have been
there and not enjoyed the experience. I have always found
Belfast exciting and often wondered why that should be. I
think I have come up with an answer. Clearly there is an
element of purely nervous excitement at seeing armed
soldiers around the place, and indeed the strange paradox
of seeing the security forces equipped for action is that it
tends to make you feel less secure yourself. There has also
been, I admit, a rather more base component to my excitement, that as a young journalist I was reporting back
from the war zone, from the front line as it were – with all
the bogus glamour the experience generates first time
around.

But the real reason why Belfast is genuinely exciting does, I think, go deeper than that. It is a place where life is lived as if it really mattered. Decisions here are important and never lightly taken; choices are hard. People in Belfast are generally "in the know"; they are involved in life, not passive victims of it. Whatever they eventually decide to do they do it with abandon and with a passion, and friendships are all the sweeter for it, enmity all the keener. It is exciting knowing that people are living on the hard edge of things that really count.

It is also worthwhile saying that I find Belfast a beautiful city – a strange description for places as superficially drab as the Ardoyne, and the Divis, the Shankill and Castlereagh. But the beauty has less to do with their physical presence than with the spirit which they and the people generate. Belfast is indeed a beautiful city; it has the terrible, painful beauty of a city where truth is fighting for its life.

Also available in Fount Paperbacks

BOOKS BY C. S. LEWIS

Reflections on the Psalms

'Absolutely packed with wisdom. It is clearly the fruit of very much reflection . . . upon one's own darkness of spirit, one's own fumbling and grasping in the shadows of prayer or of penitence.'

Trevor Huddleston

Miracles

'This is a brilliant book, abounding in lucid exposition and illuminating metaphor.'

Charles Davey, The Observer

The Problem of Pain

'Written with clarity and force, and out of much knowledge and experience.'

Times Literary Supplement

Surprised by Joy

'His outstanding gift is clarity. You can take it at two levels, as straight autobiography, or as a kind of spiritual thriller, a detective's probing of clue and motive . . .'

Isabel Quigley, Sunday Times

Hope and Suffering
Desmond Tutu

"Here . . . is the authentic voice of Christian prophecy in our day. Unafraid to proclaim . . . the truth about apartheid . . . to challenge . . . the assault on human rights . . . to risk the consequences for himself . . . But always in hope: always in love: always in the certainty that God is present . . ."

Trevor Huddleston

Naught for Your Comfort
Trevor Huddleston

The book that foretold the Soweto uprising and stirred the conscience of the world . . .

Instrument of Thy Peace
Alan Paton

"Worthy of a permanent place on the short shelf of enduring classics of the life of the Spirit."

Henry P. Van Dusan,
Union Theological Seminary

Let My People Go
Albert Luthuli

"Luthuli's love for his country transcends his loyalty to any one racial group within it. This book will surely convince the world that the Nobel Prize was most justly awarded to its author."

Trevor Huddleston

Fount Paperbacks

Fount is one of the leading paperback publishers of religious books
and below are some of its recent titles.

- [ ] THE WAY OF THE CROSS Richard Holloway   £1.95
- [ ] LIKE WIND ON THE GRASSES Rita Snowden   £1.95
- [ ] AN INTRODUCTION TO MARITAL
      PROBLEMS Jack Dominian   £2.50
- [ ] I AM WITH YOU John Woolley   £2.95
- [ ] NOW AND FOR EVER Anne Townsend   £1.95
- [ ] THE PERFECTION OF LOVE Tony Castle   £2.95
- [ ] A PROPHETIC PEOPLE Clifford Hill   £2.95
- [ ] THOMAS MORE Richard Marius   £7.95
- [ ] WALKING IN THE LIGHT David Winter   £1.95
- [ ] HALF WAY Jim Thompson   £2.50
- [ ] THE HEART OF THE BIBLE George Appleton   £4.95
- [ ] I BELIEVE Trevor Huddleston   £1.75
- [ ] PRESENT CONCERNS C. S. Lewis   £1.95
- [ ] PSALMS OF PRAISE Frances Hogan   £2.50
- [ ] MOTHER TERESA: CONTEMPLATIVE IN THE
      HEART OF THE WORLD Angelo Devananda   £2.50
- [ ] IN THE HURRICANE Adrian Hastings   £2.50

All Fount paperbacks are available at your bookshop or newsagent,
or they can be ordered by post from Fount Paperbacks, Cash Sales
Department, G.P.O. Box 29, Douglas, Isle of Man. Please send
purchase price plus 22p per book, maximum postage £3. Customers
outside the UK send purchase price, plus 22p per book. Cheque,
postal order or money order. No currency.

NAME (Block letters) _____

ADDRESS_____

_____

_____